Henry Munroe
Company C

Charles H. Arnum
Company E

William J. Netson
Company E

Alexander H. Johnson
Company C

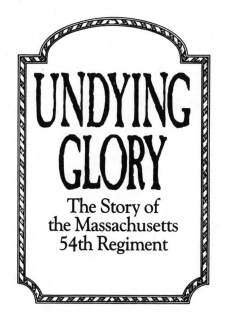

UNDYING GLORY

The Story of
the Massachusetts
54th Regiment

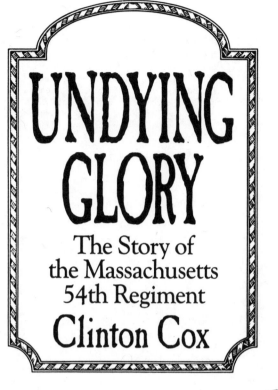

UNDYING GLORY

The Story of the Massachusetts 54th Regiment

Clinton Cox

SCHOLASTIC
HARDCOVER

Scholastic Inc.
New York

Photo Credits

Cover: Courtesy of the Library of Congress, Collection of F H. Meserve. Endpapers: All photos courtesy of the Massachusetts Historical Society. Frontispiece: Courtesy of the Historical Society of Pennsylvania. Insert: Photos 1, 8, 9, 10, and 14 courtesy of the Massachusetts Historical Society. Photo 2 courtesy of the Schlesinger Library, Radcliffe College. Photos 3 and 13 courtesy of the U.S. Army Military History Institute. Photo 4 courtesy of Howard University. Photos 5 and 12 courtesy of the Library of Congress. Photo 6 courtesy of the U.S. Army. Photo 7 courtesy of the New York Historical Society. Photo 11 courtesy of the New York Public Library. Photo 15 courtesy of Harper's Weekly. Photo 16 courtesy of the U.S. Department of Interior.

Copyright © 1991 by Clinton Cox.
All rights reserved. Published by Scholastic Inc.
SCHOLASTIC HARDCOVER is a registered trademark
of Scholastic Inc.

Library of Congress Cataloging-in-Publication Data
Cox, Clinton.
 Undying glory / Clinton Cox.
  p. cm.
 Summary: Describes the formation of the all-black 54th Massachusetts Regiment and its valiant battle history from 1863 to 1865.

 ISBN 0-590-44170-1

 1. United States. Army. Infantry Regiment, 54th (1863–1865)—History—Juvenile literature. 2. United States—History—Civil War, 1861–1865—Regimental histories—Juvenile literature.
 3. United States—History—Civil War, 1861–1865—Afro-Americans—Juvenile literature. 4. Massachusetts—History—Civil War, 1861–1865—Regimental histories—Juvenile literature.
 5. Massachusetts—History—Civil War, 1861–1865—Afro-Americans—Juvenile literature. [1. United States. Army. Infantry Regiment, 54th (1863–1865)—History. 2. United States—History—Civil War, 1861–1865—Regimental histories. 3. United States—History–Civil War, 1861–1865—Afro-Americans.] I. Title.
 E513.5 54th.C68   1991
 973.7'444—dc20   90-22303
                                                                      CIP

12 11 10 9 8 7 6 5 4 3 2   2 3 4 5 6/9

Printed in the U.S.A.   37
First Scholastic printing, October 1991

Table of Contents

For Gramps and Granny, and the love they gave us.
For Katie and Jessie, and the love they bring us.

Acknowledgements:

Writing about the 54th was like finding people who had never been allowed to tell their story, and then helping them tell it. Along the way I was aided by many people, including staff members at the National Archives, Library of Congress, New York State Library, and Oberlin College Library. Most helpful of all were the following members of the Schenectady County Public Library staff, whose professional skills were always cheerfully given: Bruce Adams, Judy Fitzmaurice, Bertha Kriegler, Andrew Kulmatiski, Timothy McGowan, and Bob Sullivan. Most of all, I would like to thank my wife, Anita, for her unfaltering help and encouragement.

The Unsung Heroes

Paul Laurence Dunbar

A song for the unsung heroes who rose in
the country's need,
When the life of the land was threatened
by the slaver's cruel greed,
For the men who came from the corn field,
who came from the plough and the flail,
Who rallied round when they heard the
sound of the mighty man of the rail.

A song for the unsung heroes who stood
the awful test,
When the humblest host that the land
could boast went forth to meet the
best;
A song for the unsung heroes who fell on
the bloody sod,
Who fought their way from night to day
and struggled up to God.

MEN OF COLOR, TO ARMS! NOW OR NEVER!

This is our Golden Moment. The Government of the United States calls for every Able-Bodied Colored Man to enter the Army for the **THREE YEARS' SERVICE,** and join in fighting the Battles of Liberty and the Union. A new era is open to us. For generations we have suffered under the horrors of slavery, outrage and wrong; our manhood has been denied, our citizenship blotted out, our souls seared and burned, our spirits cowed and crushed, and the hopes of the future of our race involved in doubts and darkness. But now the whole aspect of our relations to the white race is changed. Now therefore is our most precious moment. Let us Rush to Arms! **Fail Now and Our Race is Doomed** on this the soil of our birth. We must now awake, arise, or be forever fallen. If we value Liberty, if we wish to be free in this land, if we love our country, if we love our families, our children, our homes, we must strike NOW while the Country calls: must rise up in the dignity of our manhood, and show by our own right arms that we are worthy to be freemen. Our enemies have made the country believe that we are craven cowards, without soul, without manhood, without the spirit of soldiers. Shall we die with this stigma resting on our graves? Shall we leave this inheritance of shame to our children? No! A thousand times No! **We WILL Rise!** The alternative is upon us; let us rather die freemen than live to be slaves. What is life without liberty? We say that we have manhood—now is the time to prove it. A nation or a people that cannot fight may be pitied, but cannot be respected. If we would be regarded *Men,* if we would forever **SILENCE THE TONGUE OF CALUMNY,** of prejudice and hate; let us rise NOW and fly to arms! We have seen what **Valor and Heroism** our brothers displayed at **PORT HUDSON and at MILLIKEN'S BEND;** though they are just from the galling, poisoning grasp of slavery, they have startled the world by the most exalted heroism. If they have proved themselves heroes, can not we prove ourselves men? **ARE FREEMEN LESS BRAVE THAN SLAVES?** More than a Million White Men have left Comfortable Homes and joined the Armies of the Union to save their Country; cannot we leave ours, and swell the hosts of the Union, to save our liberties, vindicate our manhood, and deserve well of our Country?

MEN OF COLOR! All Races of Men—the Englishman, the Irishman, the Frenchman, the German, the American, have been called to assert their claim to freedom and a manly character, by an appeal to the sword. The day that has seen an enslaved race in arms, has, in all history, seen their last trial. We can now see that **OUR LAST OPPORTUNITY HAS COME!** If we are not lower in the scale of humanity than Englishmen, Irishmen, white Americans and other races, we can show it now.

MEN OF COLOR! BROTHERS and FATHERS! WE APPEAL TO YOU! By all your concern for yourselves and your liberties, by all your regard for God and Humanity, by all your desire for Citizenship and Equality before the law, by all your love for the Country, to stop at no subterfuges, listen to nothing that shall deter you from rallying for the Army. Come forward, and at once Enroll your Names for the **Three Years' Service. STRIKE NOW,** and you are henceforth and forever **FREEMEN!**

E. D. Bassett,	John W. Price,	Rev. J. Boulden,	John P. Burr,	Jas. R. Gordon,
Wm. D. Forten,	Augustus Dorsey,	Rev. J. Asher,	Robert Jones,	Samuel Stewart,
Frederick Douglass,	Rev. Stephen Smith,	Rev. J. C. Gibbs,	O. V. Catto,	David B. Bowser,
Wm. Whipper,	N. W. Depee,	Daniel George,	Thos. J. Dorsey,	Henry Minton,
D. D. Turner,	Dr. J. H. Wilson,	Robert M. Adger,	I. D. Cliff,	Daniel Colley,
Jas. McCrummell,	J. W. Cassey,	Henry M. Cropper,	Jacob C. White,	J. C. White, Jr.,
A. S. Cassey,	P. J. Armstrong,	Rev. J. B. Reeve,	Morris Hall,	Rev. J. P. Campbell,
A. M. Green,	J. W. Simpson,	Rev. J. A. Williams,	James Needham,	Rev. W. J. Alston,
J. W. Page,	Rev. J B. Trusty,	Rev. A. L. Stanford,	Rev. Elisha Weaver,	J. P. Johnson,
L. R. Seymour,	S. Morgan Smith,	Thomas J. Bowers,	Ebenezer Black,	Franklin Turner,
Rev. J. Underdue,	Wm. E. Gipson,	Elijah J. Davis,	Rev. Wm. T. Catto,	Jesse E. Glasgow.

1
"This Is a
White Man's War"

On April 12, 1861, the South fired on the United States garrison at Fort Sumter, South Carolina, plunging this country into the Civil War. Before it ended four years later, over one million men would be killed or wounded.

The South was determined to form a separate nation called the Confederacy, but the North was equally determined not to allow that to happen.

When President Abraham Lincoln called for the states to supply 75,000 volunteers for what most people thought would be a brief war, men throughout the North flocked to enlist in the Union Army.

Wrote one black editor: "Drums are beating, men are enlisting, companies forming, regiments marching, banners are flying."

Blacks and whites opposed to slavery saw the war

as a chance to finally end the brutal system. Men and women crowded to meetings to discuss how best to help the four million Southern slaves they thought would soon be free.

"A flame of fire seemed to run through the whole North," a Boston abolitionist said.

But while the government quickly accepted whites as soldiers, blacks were turned away.

Jacob Dodson, a black man who worked in the United States Senate and had journeyed to the Rocky Mountains and Far West as a member of three exploration parties, offered the services of "300 reliable colored free citizens of this city [Washington, D.C.] who desire to enter the service for the defense of the city."

His offer was refused by the secretary of war, Simon Cameron, who said, "This department has no intention at present to call into the service of the Government any colored soldiers."

Black men in Cleveland formed a military club and told the government they were ready to fight as their forebears did "in times of '76 and the days of 1812." The authorities rejected their offer.

When a group of black men in New York City began practicing military drills, the chief of police warned them to stop, claiming he "could not protect them from popular indignation and assault."

In Rhode Island, police officials said the drilling exercises of black men were "disorderly gatherings" and would be broken up.

One Ohio resident asked the governor, David Tod, for permission to raise a black regiment.

"Do you not know," the governor replied angrily, "that this is a *white man's* government; that white men are able to defend it and protect it, and that to enlist a negro soldier would be to drive every white man out of the service?"

In cities, towns, and villages throughout the free states, black men offered their services as soldiers. The answer was virtually the same everywhere: "No, this is a white man's war."

Black leaders pleaded in vain for their people to be allowed to serve, and help bring an end to slavery. The black abolitionist, ex-slave, and newspaper publisher, Frederick Douglass, appealed to "the imperilled nation to unchain against her foes her powerful black hand."

Douglass wrote, "Once let the black man get upon his person the brass letters, U.S.; let him get an eagle on his button, and a musket on his shoulder and bullets in his pocket, and there is no power on earth which can deny that he has earned the right to citizenship in the United States."

Governor John Andrew of Massachusetts, who had been fighting for years to end slavery, said, "It is not my opinion that our generals, when any man comes to the standard and desires to defend the flag, will find it important to light a candle, and see what his complexion is, or to consult the family Bible to ascertain whether his grandfather came from the banks of the Thames or the banks of the Senegal."

But men like Douglass and Andrew were in the minority. Few Americans, North or South, favored the idea of arming black men when the Civil War began. The majority did not even want to end slavery, but simply wanted to bring the Southern states back into the Union and leave slavery intact.

Slaveowners had always vigorously opposed the use of firearms by black people, and Southern states had laws making it a crime punishable by death for them to possess weapons of any kind.

The attitude of Northerners was not much different. Black residents were barred from voting in most states and from joining the militia in all states. In the years leading up to the Civil War, Indiana, Illinois, and Iowa passed laws making it a crime for blacks to move into those states. Blacks who moved there anyway were subject to severe penalties, including being sold into slavery.

Even the right to attend schools was denied to black children in most communities, though there were exceptions.

Racial violence was a routine fact of life. Competition for jobs between free blacks and newly arrived European immigrants led to many anti-black riots in large Northern cities.

Black and white abolitionists believed that public attitudes toward black people would improve dramatically if they were allowed to prove their courage on the battlefield. But most Americans did not want to give them that opportunity.

When Douglass, Governor Andrew, and others urged the use of black soldiers, President Lincoln replied that to do so "would turn 50,000 bayonets from the loyal Border States against us that are for us."

The border states, which included Delaware, Maryland, Kentucky, Missouri, and the counties in Virginia that would soon become the state of West Virginia were loyal to the Union, but also practiced slavery. Lincoln did not want to make them so angry that they would join the Confederacy. Lincoln was also afraid that white soldiers would refuse to fight if blacks were allowed to join the army.

"The people are not prepared for it," he said.

Pro-slavery sentiment was so widespread in the North at the beginning of the war that many Union generals allowed slaveowners to come into their camps and seize escaped slaves.

Union officers, said one man, "performed the disgusting duty of slave dogs. . . ."

Captain Robert Gould Shaw of the 2nd Massachusetts Infantry Regiment, future commander of the 54th Massachusetts Volunteer ("Glory") Regiment, was forced to follow army policy and return escaped slaves when he served in Virginia.

Shaw, the son of abolitionists, was deeply troubled

by this painful duty. An outraged Governor Andrew denounced the policy and said, "Massachusetts does not send her citizens forth to become the hunters of men."

Many Union soldiers, however, were more than happy to serve as slavecatchers.

Colonel Thomas Higginson, a friend of the Shaw family and of Governor Andrew, said that if the slaves had attempted an armed revolt "a large part of our army would have joined with the Southern army to hunt them down."

When the Union Army pushed into Virginia, General George B. McClellan issued a proclamation assuring slaveowners that "not only will we abstain from interfering with your slaves, but we will, on the contrary, with an iron hand, crush any attempt at insurrection on their part." McClellan also banished a popular singing group, the Hutchinson family, from camps under his command for singing anti-slavery songs.

A few generals felt just the opposite, however. One of these, Major General David Hunter, issued a proclamation in May 1862, freeing all slaves under his command. On the same day he began to recruit and arm the slaves into a regiment. Hunter had not discussed his plans with President Lincoln, though, and the president rejected the proclamation. He also said he would accept blacks only as laborers in the army, not as soldiers.

Hunter was forced to disband his regiment after

three months. None of the soldiers had been paid,
but a few months later some of the men became part
of an officially recognized regiment, the 1st South
Carolina Infantry.

Lieutenant Charles Adams, Jr., serving with a
Massachusetts cavalry unit under Hunter's command, wrote his father that the breakup of the black
regiment "was hailed here with great joy, for our
troops have become more anti-negro than I could
have imagined."

The government's policy toward enlisting black
soldiers was gradually changing, however, because
of the failure of Lincoln's attempts to compromise
with the South by promising not to interfere with
slavery. In addition, the Union faced a steadily wors-
ening military situation, and an increasing manpower shortage.

Lincoln used what he called "the simplest knowledge of arithmetic" to argue that if black men were
not allowed to enlist, "all the white men of the
North" would be sacrificed in the war.

By early 1862, an average of 60,000 Union soldiers
were sick every day and the death rate from disease
was costing the army the equivalent of 27 regiments
a year. McClellan's attempt to capture the Confederate capitol at Richmond failed, when General Robert E. Lee stopped him in the Battle of Seven Days
(June 25–July 1). Union troops were also defeated at
Bull Run and were driven back when they attempted
to capture Vicksburg, Mississippi. The capture of

Vicksburg would have given the Union control of the vital Mississippi River.

Sixty-five thousand soldiers were due for discharge in the summer and fall, and Northerners had almost ceased volunteering for the army. Many governors were having trouble filling their quotas with whites and hoped to enlist blacks instead.

In a letter to Secretary of War Edwin Stanton, Governor Andrew predicted that if Lincoln would allow blacks to enlist, "the roads will swarm, if need be, with multitudes whom New England would pour out to obey your call."

The North, quite simply, was running out of men able and willing to fight, and the only remaining source of untapped manpower was black men.

Many war-weary white soldiers and their families had also decided it would be in their best interests if blacks did some of the dying. An army captain from Illinois urged the government to recruit blacks because it was this country's duty "to protect the lives of its white citizens. And the Government will be weakened less by the loss of three negroes than it would by the loss of one white man."

Lincoln had earlier considered issuing a proclamation freeing the slaves, but had rejected the idea because he was "afraid that half the officers would fling down their arms and three more states would rise [rebel]."

By the summer of 1862, though, he was quietly making plans that would lead to the acceptance of blacks in the army. In July he told his cabinet he was going to issue a proclamation freeing all slaves in those states still fighting against the Union on January 1, 1863.

Secretary of State William Seward suggested that the president wait to issue the proclamation until Union armies had scored a battlefield victory.

Otherwise, Seward said, it would look like "a cry of help" from the government to blacks, asking them to save the Union, rather than the other way around: "The government stretching forth her hands to Ethiopia instead of Ethiopia stretching forth her hands to the government."

Lincoln agreed and waited for the proper time. It came on September 22, five days after the battle of Antietam in Maryland, where almost 6,000 men were killed and 17,000 wounded in five hours. Captain Shaw fought there and later said the horrible bloodshed made him doubt his ability to be courageous in battle.

Though Antietam was far from a clear-cut victory, Lincoln issued his preliminary proclamation. Then, on January 1, he issued the final version of the Emancipation Proclamation.

The president called it a "necessary war measure for suppressing said rebellion." It did not free slaves in the border states, because those states had remained loyal to the Union.

The proclamation contained a paragraph black Americans had long awaited: a declaration that freed slaves "of suitable condition" would be "received into the armed service of the United States, to garrison forts, positions, stations, and other places, and to man vessels of all sorts in said service."

Black men could now enlist in the Union Army, though most military officials intended to use them primarily as laborers and guards rather than combat soldiers.

At last the door of opportunity was open. The Emancipation Proclamation was celebrated throughout the North and by blacks in those parts of the South that had been freed by Union troops.

Charlotte Forten, a black teacher from Massachusetts who had established a school for the children of ex-slaves on the Sea Islands of South Carolina, wrote in her diary: "The most glorious day this nation has yet seen, I think."

January 1 had traditionally been known as "Heart-Break Day" by black Americans in slavery because it meant the sale of their loved ones, who would probably never be seen again. But, after Lincoln issued his proclamation of freedom, wrote one man, the day was given "new significance and imperishable glory in the calendar of time."

Frederick Douglass again called for black men to enlist "and smite with death the power that would bury the Government and your liberty in the same hopeless grave." Probably remembering his own days as a slave, when it seemed that slavery would never end, Douglass cried: "From east to west, from north to south the sky is written all over with 'now or never.' "

Almost before the ink was dry on the proclamation, Governor Andrew was in Washington seeking permission to raise a black regiment in North Carolina. That idea was rejected and he then asked for authority to recruit black troops for a regiment from Massachusetts.

On January 26, Secretary of War Stanton issued an order giving him permission "to raise such numbers of volunteer companies of artillery for duty in the forts of Massachusetts and elsewhere, and such corps of infantry for the volunteer military service as he may find convenient, such volunteers to be enlisted for three years, or until sooner discharged, and may include persons of African descent, organized into special corps."

Four days later Andrew wrote to Captain Shaw's father, asking him to speak to his 25-year-old son about accepting command of the unit.

The governor said he wanted officers "of firm anti-slavery principles, ambitious, superior to a vulgar contempt for color, and having faith in the capacity of colored men for military service."

Shaw's father personally carried the letter to his son in Virginia. Captain Shaw, a family friend later pointed out, "was sure of promotion where he stood. In this new negro-soldier venture, loneliness was certain, ridicule inevitable, failure possible . . . and, although he had stood among the bullets at Cedar

Mountain and Antietam, he had till then been walking socially on the sunny side of life. But whatever doubts may have beset him, they were over in a day. . . ."

Shaw talked the offer over with his father and close friends, then wrote a letter of refusal to the governor. But the next day he changed his mind and wired his father: "Please destroy my letter and telegraph to the governor that I accept."

To his fiancée Annie Haggerty, Shaw wrote: ". . . while I was undecided I felt ashamed of myself, as if I were a coward."

With the birth of the 54th Regiment, President Lincoln had started down a road whose end was far from clear, but he felt confident of the course. Though a few regiments had already been formed on Southern territory controlled by the Union Army, the 54th was the first one recruited in the North. It was also the first black regiment with the whole-hearted support of the government. On its conduct, a newspaper said, "depended for a long time the success of the whole experiment of arming black citizens in defence of the Republic."

The valor of its men would eventually be celebrated throughout the North and help open the door for the acceptance of black soldiers for the remaining years of the Civil War.

Before that acceptance was gained, the Union Army fought to defeat the South but not to free the slaves. After that acceptance was gained and black men fought as soldiers by the tens of thousands, the Union Army became an army for black liberation.

The men of the 54th and other black regiments were destined to provide the country with a power, Lincoln would say in a few months, that "is more than we can lose and live. Nor can we, by discarding it, get a white force in place of it."

Keep that power, Lincoln declared, "and you can save the Union. Throw it away and the Union goes with it."

But on the day Shaw wired his acceptance, the 54th consisted only of the young, soon-to-be colonel. The 1,000 men he would command had yet to be found.

2
"Men of Color, to Arms!"

Governor Andrew wasted no time, now that his dream was on the verge of coming true. On February 7, Andrew appointed John Appleton of Boston as the regiment's first recruiter.

Appleton, whom Andrew also commissioned a first lieutenant in the regiment, promptly opened an office in Boston and took out the following newspaper ad:

"TO COLORED MEN
"Wanted. Good men for the Fifty-Fourth Regiment of Massachusetts Volunteers of African descent, Col. Robert G. Shaw (commanding). $100 bounty at expiration of term of service. Pay $13 per month, and State aid for families. All necessary infor-

mation can be obtained at the office, corner
Cambridge and North Russell Streets.
                    Lieut. J.W.M. Appleton,
                    Recruiting Officer."

In the first five days Appleton recruited 25 men
and, before the office closed a few weeks later, almost
30 more. Appleton was often taunted by whites opposed to enlisting black soldiers, but by the end of
March he had enough recruits to make up the regiment's first company: Company A.

Another recruiter traveled to the old whaling
town of New Bedford, Massachusetts, which had a
sizable black population. James Grace, who was also
commissioned a first lieutenant by Andrew, opened
a recruiting office and placed the United States flag
out front.

Grace spoke to black church congregations and
arranged for Frederick Douglass, William Lloyd Garrison, and other well-known abolitionists to appear
with him to urge black men to enlist.

Grace's son was taunted in school and the lieutenant was insulted on the street because of his efforts
for the 54th, but 75 men soon joined up. These men
and others formed what became known as the regiment's Massachusetts company: Company C.

Three more recruiters traveled to Philadelphia.
The opposition to black soldiers was so powerful
there that one of the white recruiters had to personally buy each new recruit a railroad ticket. Then,

either at night, or one man at a time if it was by
daylight, he hurriedly smuggled the recruits onto a
train for Boston. These men formed the basis of
Company B.

Recruiting was proceeding too slowly for the im-
patient Andrew, however, complicated by the fact
that Massachusetts had only a small black population
to draw from. Since there was no formal recruiting
system for the army when the Civil War began, the
federal government simply told each state how many
men it wanted. It was then up to state officials to
sign up the required number.

Governor Andrew turned to an old friend, George
L. Stearns, and asked him to arrange to recruit black
men throughout the North.

Stearns promptly set up recruiting posts from Boston to St. Louis, and asked black leaders to act as
recruiting agents. Less than four weeks after Andrew
received permission from Secretary of War Edwin M.
Stanton to raise the 54th, Stearns traveled to Roch-
ester, New York, and asked Frederick Douglass for
help.

It was the best move Stearns could have made.
Three days later Douglass published an editorial in
his newspaper, *Douglass' Monthly*, urging black men
to enlist in the Union Army. His words became
famous throughout the North.

"Men of Color, to Arms!" Douglass headlined his
appeal.

"When first the rebel cannon shattered the walls

of Sumter and drove away its starving garrison, I
predicted that the war then and there inaugurated
would not be fought out entirely by white men,"
Douglass wrote. ". . . .A war undertaken and bra-
zenly carried on for the perpetual enslavement of
colored men, calls logically and loudly for colored
men to help suppress it. . . . Go quickly and help
fill up the first colored regiment from the North. I
am authorized to assure you that you will receive the
same wages, the same rations, the same equipments,
the same protection, the same treatment, and the
same bounty, secured to white soldiers."

His editorial was reprinted in newspapers throughout the North, and was eagerly discussed wherever
black people gathered.

Douglass himself also traveled tirelessly to large
cities and small, in state after state, sometimes recruiting 20 or 25, and sometimes persuading only a
handful. He even traveled to Philadelphia, despite
the hostility shown other recruiters there.

"Fred Douglass was here for three days and lectured
twice," a Philadelphia resident wrote a friend. "The
last one was on the Crisis [the war] in Bethel Church
to a mixed multitude and made an appeal for recruits
for the 54 Massachusetts Reg. but only got five. The
work goes on very privately. . . ."

In the decades leading up to the Civil War, many
Americans believed it would be impossible for free
blacks and whites to live together in the same country. As a result, various colonization organizations

sprang up with the goal to remove free blacks from this country and resettle them in Haiti, Central and South America, and Africa.

Thomas Jefferson headed a Virginia legislative committee in 1777 that proposed gradual emancipation and the colonization of those slaves who were freed. Lincoln, like many Americans in the eighteenth and nineteenth centuries, also supported such efforts and continued to call for colonization even after the war began.

In 1862 he met a group of black leaders in the White House and told them: "There is an unwillingness on the part of our people, harsh as it may be, for you free colored people to remain among us."

He asked the leaders to recruit volunteers for a government-sponsored colonization project in Central America, and the next year the U.S. transported 453 black Americans to an island near Haiti. The survivors were eventually returned to the U.S. after the group was decimated by smallpox and starvation.

Most black Americans opposed such schemes and agreed with Frederick Douglass when he angrily told Lincoln: "This is our country as much as it is yours, and we will not leave it."

One of those willing to leave it, however, was Douglass' son. Twenty-two-year-old Lewis Douglass, feeling that blacks would never be treated as equal citizens in the United States, joined with 500 other free young black men to settle in Chiriqui, in what is now Panama.

The plan was Lincoln's and it was backed by the U.S. Congress which, in July 1862, voted $20 million to resettle free blacks outside the United States. Lincoln's policy was based on his belief that Northerners would not accept the Emancipation Proclamation unless they were assured the ex-slaves would not settle in their states.

Before the plan could be carried out though, Governor Andrew announced formation of the 54th Regiment. Instead of leaving this country to search for freedom and equality, Lewis Douglass and many others joined the 54th to search for it on the battleground.

Lewis was his father's first recruit, and he was soon joined by his 19-year-old brother, Charles. Both were printers on their father's newspaper. In less than four months, Sergeant Major Lewis Douglass would fight side by side with Colonel Robert Shaw when they stormed the walls of Fort Wagner.

The federal government provided a bounty to each white soldier who volunteered to join the Union Army. There was no bounty for black volunteers, however. The Massachusetts legislature had to vote to provide the money and also to provide transportation to Boston for black recruits.

Funds for the actual recruiting, and for transportation home for those rejected, were contributed by private individuals.

Among the contributions listed for April 1863 by the recruiting committee's treasurer were the following: "U. and J. Ritchie, $50; Charles E. Allen, 50 cents; A Friend, $5; Mrs. Barstow, 3 pair socks; J. B. Whitmore, 7 barrels of apples; Rice, Kendall & Co., package of stationary."

At one point, as money was running out, George Stearns contributed thousands of dollars in addition to working 10 to 18 hours a day.

Soon the number of recruits coming into Camp Meigs, the regimental base near Boston, began to swell.

Stephen Meyer, an ex-slave and a prominent abolitionist in Albany, New York, turned over 18 recruits to Douglass.

Clarence Bromley Hoke, an 18-year-old farmer from tiny Canajoharie in upstate New York, and Charles Van Allen, a 29-year-old farmer from Lenox, Massachusetts, marched off to war.

On his seventeenth birthday, Toussaint L'Ouverture Delaney wrote from Canada asking his father for permission to join the 54th.

His father was Martin R. Delaney, a physician who would go on to become the first black officer commissioned in the Union Army, a novelist, an African explorer, and the man who is known today as the father of black nationalism.

The elder Delaney, grandson of a Mandingo prince and a Golah chief, was also a recruiter for the 54th. He read his son's letter with pride and fear, carried it in his breast pocket for a day, then wrote back giving his permission.

On March 27, 1863, Toussaint signed the muster roll of Company D as Private Delaney.

At Syracuse, 22 of the 25 men who volunteered passed the required physical examination, while Buffalo provided seven recruits.

Men responded to the call from village, town, and city; from north, south, east, and west.

James Allen, a 26-year-old railroad brakeman from Lafayette, Indiana, joined up. From Elmira, New York, came a 31-year-old boatman named Stephen Atkins Swails. Joining with them was a 20-year-old painter named Silas Garrison, who made his way to the 54th from Chatham, Canada, and a 22-year-old seaman from New Bedford named William Carney. Allen Powell, a 25-year-old blacksmith, came all the way from Front Royal, Virginia, to join up.

And from Battle Creek, Michigan, came the 19-year-old blacksmith grandson of Sojourner Truth, abolitionist, reformer, and women's rights activist. She took the name "Sojourner" because she was "to travel up and down the land" fighting injustice, and "Truth" because the word stood for God, whose voice she said she often heard.

Her grandson, who had been her constant companion since he was a child, signed the regimental muster roll as Private James Caldwell of Company H.

By the middle of April, Douglass had sent more than 100 recruits to Boston, and agents in other states had been just as busy. This was especially true in Ohio.

Before Governor Andrew received permission to raise the 54th, Martin Delaney had asked the first president of Ohio's Oberlin College to sponsor an all-black army division. The college president, Asa Mahan, asked authorities in Washington for permission, but was turned down.

Many Oberlin citizens had participated in what would go down in local legend as the Oberlin-Wellington rescue. On January 1, 1859, 200 to 300 townspeople and college students raced nine miles to Wellington and rescued a young fugitive slave about to be returned to the South.

Several of the rescuers were later arrested and tried in federal court for violating the Fugitive Slave Act, which required that all citizens of the United States help return escaped slaves to the slaveowners.

John Mercer Langston's brother-in-law, O.S.B. Wall, and Langston's brother, Charles, were two of those who were tried on the charge of "rescuing." Wall was found not guilty, while Charles was found guilty and served twenty days in jail.

With Wall and John Langston acting as recruiters, Oberlin sent more men to the 54th than all but the largest cities.

Langston was apparently the first black man elected to public office in the United States, winning the office of town clerk in a small community northwest of Oberlin in 1855. The son of a slaveowner, he was freed when his father died and went on to become dean of Howard University after the war and a United States congressman.

Wall's white father was also a slaveowner, and his sisters and brothers were freed when their father died. Their father willed them land he owned in Ohio, and most of the family moved to Oberlin after his death.

Wall's first recruits were his cousins, Albert and John Wall, both 20 years old. Albert was a tailor and John was a student in Oberlin College's preparatory department.

On April 3, 1863, they left Oberlin along with several other recruits, including a 25-year-old shoemaker named Henry Peal. Peal was born in Richmond, Virginia, and may have been an escaped slave. In the months preceding his enlistment, he attended a school in Oberlin for former slaves.

Another Oberlin recruit was 21-year-old Benjamin Green. His grandfather was a Narragansett Indian who fought with the Massachusetts militia in the Revolutionary War, 87 years before his grandson journeyed to Massachusetts to fight another war for freedom.

Local townspeople gave each of the recruits four dollars and a New Testament as they marched off to war amid the cheers of their neighbors.

Nothing could have shown more clearly the changed attitudes in the North toward the enlistment of black men as soldiers than a letter sent by Ohio's Governor Tod to Governor Andrew.

Tod, completely reversing his earlier stand against

allowing blacks in the army, wrote Andrew: "Dear
Sir: You are already aware of the fact that the military
authorities of Ohio are doing what they can to stim-
ulate enlistments within the State for your brigade
of colored men. I have heretofore requested of you
to cause the colored men from Ohio to be organized,
so far as practicable, into companies by themselves,
with which request I doubt not, your Excellency will
cheerfully comply."

Andrew agreed, and most of the soldiers from
Ohio were placed in Companies G, I, and K.

On the same day Tod wrote to Andrew, he also
wrote to John Langston in Oberlin: "I am glad to
know that you are devoting your best energies to the
work of raising troops for this brigade, and trust your
efforts will be highly successful."

Langston and Wall, who was later commissioned
a captain in the Union Army, both went on to recruit and organize black soldiers in several states in
the South. But for now their efforts were focused on
the 54th and the 18 men they had just sent from
Oberlin to the camp at Readville.

Time was passing quickly for the Union Army with
its desperate need for men, and Union generals
wanted new recruits in the field as soon as possible.

The first 72 men arrived in the cold of February
at an almost deserted camp, but others soon followed. They came "with a steady and increasing
flow," wrote one of the officers, "singly, in squads,
and even in detachments from the several agencies
established throughout the country."

By the end of April, less than three months after recruiting first began, the roster of the 54th was filled. On May 13, barely 13 weeks since Appleton — who'd been promoted from lieutenant to captain — recruited the first men, the last of the regiment's ten companies was officially sworn in.

Governor Andrew was determined to make the regiment a success, so all those wishing to join were given unusually stringent physicals. One third were rejected, with the result that the regiment was physically far above average.

"A more robust, strong, and healthy set of men were never mustered into the service of the United States," wrote Massachusetts' Surgeon General William Dale.

And so 1,000 young men were now ready to begin the training that would carry them into battle, risking their lives and freedom to help liberate four million slaves.

A thousand eager, would-be soldiers came seeking the dream of freedom for those who had never known it.

They came with hope in their hearts to a barren campground outside of Boston in the darkness of mid-winter.

At last their journey had begun.

3
"The Colored Man's Flag"

The recruits came from 22 states, the District of Columbia, Nova Scotia and the West Indies. Sixty-eight men came from Philadelphia, 47 from Boston, 11 from New York City, 20 from Chicago, and one each from over one hundred villages and towns most people had never heard of.

Twenty-one-year-old James McCloud, a seaman, made his way to the regiment from St. Thomas in the West Indies and Robert J. Simmons came all the way from Bermuda.

Many were the only financial support their families had and knew they might never return to their loved ones again, or they might return maimed for life. They also knew they faced being murdered if captured or, perhaps even worse, sold into slavery.

But still they came, sometimes fifteen or twenty

at a time, and sometimes singly or in twos and threes.

According to one of their officers only a few of the men had ever been slaves, which made their willingness to risk enslavement all the more impressive.

The largest occupation groups were laborers (402) and farmers (344), just as these were usually the largest occupation groups in white regiments. But there were dozens of other occupations as well, from boatmen and barbers to seamen and stonecutters. Five were listed as engineers, four were students, and one was a dentist.

There was even an artist, Company I's 32-year-old Grimms Z. Smith of Boston, and a druggist, Company G's 25-year-old William Underwood of Mason County, Kentucky.

Many of the recruits were described as "light-complexioned," with the rest said to be "brown" or "dark." The largest group of recruits (765) were in their 20s, but there were also nine 16-year-olds and 39 men in their 40s. The oldest member of the 54th was Henry Craig of Company K, a 47-year-old boatman from Cincinnati, Ohio.

The average age of the officers was 23.

The educational level was higher in the 54th than in many white regiments. Shaw wrote his fiancée, Annie Haggerty, that of 38 recruits who had come into camp from New Bedford, "there are only two who cannot read or write."

Officers in other regiments frequently complained

that there were not enough literate enlisted men to fill such jobs as clerks and noncommissioned officers. But in the 54th, according to one officer, there were enough "to more than supply all requirements for warrant officers and clerks."

The mustering officer, who was from Virginia, told Shaw he had "never mustered in so fine a set of men, though about 20,000 have passed through his hands since September."

The regiment's officers, all of whom were white, were also carefully selected, not only for their competence as soldiers, but for their feelings toward black people.

Officers for white troops in the Civil War were normally chosen because of how many they recruited or how popular they were with the troops.

Governor Andrew knew, however, that the 54th would largely stand or fall on the competence and attitude of its officers. He therefore handpicked the officers, choosing most from prominent abolitionist families.

"The officers and men are both carefully picked," he wrote Secretary Stanton in April. "We have aimed at getting officers of high character, making careful selections out of many candidates."

He and Shaw picked Edward N. Hallowell as assistant commander, and Francis L. Higginson, Cabot J. Russel, and John W. Appleton as three of the ten company commanders. All belonged to distinguished abolitionist families.

Andrew told a friend he had sometimes accepted officers for white regiments who were rough and uncultivated, "but these men shall be commanded by officers who are eminently gentlemen."

Typical of the commitment shown by the men who became officers in the 54th was that of William H. Simpkins, originally a member of the 44th Massachusetts Infantry.

"I have to tell you of a pretty important step that I have just taken," Simpkins wrote a friend. "I have given my name to be forwarded to Massachusetts for a commission in the Fifty-fourth Negro Regiment, Colonel Shaw. This is no hasty conclusion, no blind leap of an enthusiast, but the result of much hard thinking. It will not be at first, and probably not for a long time, an agreeable position, for many reasons too evident to state . . . but it is an experiment that I think it high time we should try. . . ."

Andrew also tried to get permission from the War Department to commission black officers.

On February 3, even before receiving authority to raise the 54th, Andrew had told Secretary Stanton that the law "does not prohibit Colored officers in colored Regiments. Will you withdraw prohibition so far as concerns line officers, assistant Surgeons & Chaplain of my proposed Colored Regiment. It will avoid difficulty. Power would not be used except possibly for few cases of plainly competent persons, recommended by the field officers . . ."

A few days later he sent another telegram saying,

"My discretion may be trusted. The mere power will be useful."

But Stanton and President Lincoln were both afraid that many whites, who saw the enlistment of black soldiers as the first step toward racial and political equality, would violently oppose any moves to make them officers.

The issue also stirred the emotions of black Americans, with many opposing enlistment until the government allowed them to receive commissions.

Abolitionists argued against that view, saying it was important for blacks to seize the opportunity to prove themselves on the battlefield. Once that was done, they said, the commissions would follow.

"Is it not ridiculous in us all at once refusing to be commanded by white men in time of war, when we are everywhere commanded by white men in time of peace?" asked Douglass.

Most black Americans agreed with Douglass, and felt the racial barriers would fall once they proved their valor.

And so the regiment began to drill for the battles soon to come: 1,000 black men and 29 white officers.

Even before all the men were in camp, a contented Shaw wrote: "Everything goes on prosperously. The intelligence of the men is a great surprise to me. They learn all the details of guard duty and camp service infinitely more readily than most of the Irish I have had under my command."

Many Civil War regiments suffered high disease

rates because of poor sanitary conditions, and the men often went for weeks without taking a bath or washing their clothes. As a result, it was not unusual for new regiments to have two thirds of their men on sick call.

A report for the U.S. Sanitary Commission described a typical camp: "Camp streets and spaces between the tents littered with refuse, food and other rubbish, sometimes in an offensive state of decomposition; slops deposited in pits within the camp limits or thrown out broadcast; heaps of manure and offal close to the camp."

The result was that more men died of diarrhea and disease during the war than were killed in combat. The 54th's Camp Meigs was a pleasant contrast to all this, however.

"The barracks, cook-houses, and kitchens far surpassed in cleanliness any I have ever witnessed, and were models of neatness and good order," reported Surgeon General Dale.

Dale also said there was "less drunkenness in this regiment than in any that had ever left Massachusetts . . ."

The soldiers were also praised for their eagerness in learning how to drill and handle weapons. Many had trained on their own as soon as the war began, hoping the government would one day allow them to fight.

The men lived in large barracks, which were heated by wood fires, and in bad weather they drilled

in the barracks. A few recruits died of pneumonia
and bronchitis during February and March, but the
death and disease rate was lower than for most
regiments.

Every Sunday visitors flocked to the camp to watch
the soldiers, and on April 2 the first dress parade
took place. The men looked striking in the blue
uniforms of the United States Army. Shaw had to
fight for their right to wear the regulation uniforms,
rather than clownlike uniforms with red stripes some
army officials tried to give them.

On April 30 the men formed in regimental lines
for the first time. Governor Andrew and Secretary
of the Treasury Salmon P. Chase, a lawyer who had
defended many runaway slaves before the war began,
watched proudly as the 54th marched by.

That same day the officers were issued swords and
the enlisted men received Enfield muskets. The
muskets weighed about 14 pounds each and could
only be fired once before reloading, a cumbersome
process that took 40–45 seconds. In the heat of
battle that was a long time, and soldiers generally
had to fight with their bayonets after getting off only
one or two shots.

By May 11, the regiment was full and just one
week later came the 54th's most memorable day so
far: presentation of the flags the unit would carry
into battle.

Special trains were run to the camp, and over
3,000 visitors thronged the parade ground. There

was Governor Andrew, whose dream had done so much to make the 54th a reality. There was Frederick Douglass, who escaped from slavery at the age of 20 and devoted the rest of his life to freeing those still enslaved.

There was William Lloyd Garrison, who had once been dragged through the streets of Boston at the end of a rope by a mob intent on lynching him because of his anti-slavery activities. And there was Wendell Phillips who, at 26, turned his back on a privileged life of wealth and dedicated himself to the abolition of slavery. The eloquence of his speeches, said one man who knew him, helped "melt the fetters from a race and transform a nation."

These men, like the rest of the crowd of black and white, young and old, must have felt hopes and dreams too powerful for words as they watched the men of the 54th perform their drills.

There were four flags to be presented: the flag of the United States; the Massachusetts flag; a flag of white silk with a figure of the Goddess of Liberty and the motto, "Liberty, Loyalty, and Unity"; and a blue flag with a white cross and the Latin words, "In Hoc Signo Vinces" — "With This Sign Thou Shalt Conquer."

Governor Andrew presented the flags to Colonel Shaw on what one participant called a "fine and cloudless" day.

The flags were more than ornaments. They were carried into battle by men who stayed as close to the front of the attack as they could, showing their comrades the way they should go by holding the flag high. Flag-bearers suffered some of the highest casualty rates of the war, and sometimes the smoke on a battlefield was so thick the flag was all that could be seen.

"Wherever its folds shall be unfurled, it will mark the path of glory," the governor said to Shaw as he handed him the American flag. ". . . You will never part with that flag so long as a splinter of the staff or a thread of its web remains within your grasp."

Then, looking out over the long lines of armed black men in the shape of a huge square, Andrew declared: "I know not, Mr. Commander, when, in all human history, to any given thousand men in arms there has been committed a work at once so proud, so precious, so full of hope and glory as the work committed to you."

Henry Peal, now a corporal, was picked to carry the Massachusetts flag for the regiment. John Wall, his friend, was chosen to carry the flag of the United States.

"It makes me proud that two of the Oberlin boys carry the first flags that ever the Colored man could call his country's flag," Peal wrote to his hometown newspaper.

On May 2, Shaw found time to marry Annie Haggerty in New York City, then enjoy a brief honeymoon on his father-in-law's farm.

"Indeed, one reason for my wishing to be married is that we are going to undertake a very dangerous piece of work, and I feel that there are more chances than ever of my not getting back," Shaw wrote his mother, who initially objected to the marriage.

Those few days were all Shaw and Annie would have as husband and wife, for immediately after the presentation of the flags, Governor Andrew handed him a telegram from Secretary Stanton:

"THE FIFTY FOURTH MASSACHUSETTS WILL REPORT TO GENERAL HUNTER. MAKE REQUISITIONS, SO THAT THEY MAY GO AT ONCE."

General Hunter, who had tried unsuccessfully to form the regiment of ex-slaves in South Carolina in 1862, wanted the 54th under his command at Hilton Head, South Carolina.

The regiment hurriedly prepared to leave.

On May 28, at 6:30 A.M., the men lined up and marched to the Readville train station. At 9 A.M. they arrived in Boston where they would embark for the South on a ship called the *De Molay*.

New York officials had warned Andrew not to send the 54th through their city because of racial tensions. Officials were also uncertain of the reception the troops would receive in Boston, so they held a large police force out of sight along the line of march in case there was a riot. But there was no riot that day.

Cheering spectators lined the route, waving a sea

of flags. People jammed balconies and windows watching the 54th march forth, in the words of one man, "to blot out with their own blood the sin of the nation."

Shaw led the way astride his horse, leading the regiment through winding narrow streets to Boston Common. There they halted for a review by the governor and his staff. Then, after a brief rest, they resumed their march toward Battery Wharf.

"Vast crowds lined the streets where the regiment was to pass, and the Common was crowded with an immense number of people such as only the Fourth of July or some rare event causes to assemble," one paper reported.

The jubilant spectators joined in singing "John Brown's Marching Song":

> ". . . He shall file in front where the
>   lines of battle form —
> He shall face to front when the squares of
>   battle form —
> Time with the column, and charge with
>   the storm,
> Where men are marching on. . . ."

All the while the long column of troops passed by, rifles glinting in the sun. The men marched over ground stained by the blood of Crispus Attucks, a black man who was the first American killed by the British in the American Revolution. They marched through streets where, 11 years before, United States soldiers dragged a fugitive slave past silent throngs to a ship that would take him back to slavery.

That slave, Thomas Sims, eventually returned to Boston as a free man and stood in the crowd that day watching the 54th march by.

Thunderous applause and shouts marked the soldiers' every step. Flags and handkerchiefs waved wherever the men appeared, and many of the soldiers' wives and sweethearts ran beside them.

That night poet Henry Wadsworth Longfellow, an ardent abolitionist, wrote in his diary: "Saw the first regiment of blacks march through Beacon Street. An imposing sight, with something wild and strange about it, like a dream. At last the North consents to let the Negro fight for freedom."

About one in the afternoon the regiment began to board the steamer. Guns were placed in boxes and carried on, then the officers' horses were loaded. At 4 P.M. the lines were cast off and the *De Molay* moved slowly from the wharf. A few visitors remained on board, but a tugboat soon took them off and returned them to Boston.

By nightfall the men of the 54th were well out to sea on their way to South Carolina and war. None of the men had been in uniform more than three months. Undoubtedly their thoughts were of the homes and loved ones they had left behind and of the battles yet to come.

And perhaps, as they drifted off to sleep that first

night on a journey that had already brought them so far, they thought of words Governor Andrew had spoken the day he presented the flags:

"May the infinite mercy of Almighty God attend you every hour of every day through all . . . that dangerous life in which you have embarked; may the God of our fathers cover your heads in the day of battle. . . ."

4
"I Shall Burn This Town"

The men and officers of the 54th sailed from a place where most people now seemed to regard them as heroes, toward a land where they were officially considered outlaws subject to enslavement and execution.

On December 23, 1862, Confederate President Jefferson Davis had issued a proclamation classifying all black soldiers as outlaws and declaring that "all negro slaves if captured in arms be at once delivered over to the executive authorities of the respective States to which they belong, to be dealt with according to the laws of said States."

The laws in all Southern states provided for the execution of any black person found with a weapon, whether free or slave. Davis' proclamation therefore

was a direct threat to kill or enslave all captured
black soldiers.

Less than four weeks before the 54th sailed from
Boston, that threat was also extended to the regiment's white officers.

On May 1 the Confederate Congress passed a res-
olution stating that all officers captured while leading
black troops would be "deemed as inciting servile
[slave] insurrection, and shall, if captured be put to
death or otherwise punished."

A worried supporter of the 54th asked Governor
Andrew for assurances the government would give
the same protection to black soldiers it gave to
whites.

Andrew replied that Secretary Stanton told him
"in the most emphatic manner that he would never
consent that free colored men should be accepted
into the service to serve as soldiers in the South,
until he should be assured that the Government of
the United States was prepared to guarantee and
defend to the last dollar and the last man, to these
men, all the rights, privileges, and immunities that
are given by the laws of civilized warfare to other
soldiers. . . . They will be soldiers of the Union,
nothing less and nothing different."

But when a Confederate raiding party captured
four black men in Union Army uniforms the previous
November (apparently members of General Hunter's
short-lived regiment), President Davis and Confederate Secretary of War James Seddon approved their

"summary execution" in order to discourage the North from arming blacks.

Despite widespread claims that blacks were too cowardly to fight whites, the reality was that white Southerners were afraid of them.

"I have talked with numbers of Parolled Prisoners in Vicksburg," one Union officer wrote his mother, "and they all admit it was the hardest stroke that there cause has received — the arming of the negrow. Not a few of them told me that they would rather fight two Regiments of White soldiers than one of Niggers. Rebel Citizens fear them more than they would fear Indians."

"Some swift and terrible punishment should be inflicted that their fellows may be deterred from following their example," a Confederate general wrote.

Abolitionists pleaded with Lincoln to retaliate against captured Confederate soldiers to force the South to treat black soldiers according to the rules of war. But Lincoln steadfastly refused to act.

When white soldiers were threatened with execution, Douglass wrote angrily, the President immediately promised to retaliate "sternly and severely." When black soldiers were executed, however, "no word comes from the Capitol."

Douglass declared that until Lincoln gave equal protection to black soldiers "the civilized world will hold him equally responsible with Jefferson Davis" for their murders.

And so the 54th steamed south to war, black men

and white men who had been strangers short weeks before, now bound together by their common belief in freedom for all men and the threat of death or slavery for acting on that belief.

They went forth to fight, as one officer put it, "with ropes around their necks." Many of the men took a grim delight in their status, and in the fact that their officers shared it.

On June 3, five days after leaving Boston and its cheering crowds, the men on the *De Molay* watched quietly as the ship passed Confederate-held Fort Sumter where the war had begun.

Beyond the fort and the harbor that it guarded, the men could see the rooftops of Charleston, the Rebel stronghold. The city was the principal objective of that part of the Union Army the 54th was now joining.

Union ships blockaded the harbor and the several fortified islands on either side, though Confederate ships sometimes slipped in at night with their cargoes of weapons and supplies.

The 54th continued south approximately 60 more miles, passing countless little sandy islands that dotted the coast of South Carolina. Finally, at 2:30 P.M., the *De Molay* docked at Hilton Head near the Georgia border, among more than 70 frigates, gunboats, and other ships.

Shaw reported to Hunter, who ordered the regiment inland a few miles to Beaufort. There the men set up camp in an open field. Shaw rode his horse into town to look around and met Thomas Wentworth Higginson, an abolitionist and fellow Bostonian, who commanded the 1st South Carolina Volunteers. Almost all the soldiers in the 1st South Carolina were ex-slaves who had escaped to the Union lines.

Years later Higginson recalled that Shaw wondered if the men of the 54th would fight, or if he would have to put them "between two fires" to make them fight by cutting off any possibility of retreat.

Commanders in many wars have employed that tactic, often by placing armed guards in the rear whose duty was to stop soldiers from fleeing.

"I should never have thought of such a project," said Higginson, "but I could not have expected him to trust them as I did, until he had actually been under fire with them. That, doubtless, removed all his anxieties, if he really had any."

Four days later General Hunter ordered Shaw to report to Colonel James Montgomery at St. Simons Island, Georgia, about 80 miles south.

Colonel Montgomery, who commanded the post, had once lived in Kentucky and owned slaves. He was now in charge of the 2nd South Carolina Volunteers, a regiment of ex-slaves he had recruited on raids into Confederate territory.

Montgomery had earned a reputation for brutality both against Confederates and his own men. Shaw, though pleased at the prospect of action, was uncomfortable about being put under his command.

Soon after meeting him, Shaw wrote his wife that Montgomery "looks as if he would have quite a taste for hanging people, whenever a suitable subject should offer."

The men of the 54th were busy setting up their tents when a steamer carrying Montgomery appeared at the wharf. "How soon can you be ready to start off on an expedition?" Montgomery yelled to Shaw.

"In half an hour," Shaw replied.

Soon eight of the 54th's ten companies were steaming downriver on a transport to Montgomery's camp where they were joined by another transport carrying five of his companies and a section of the 3rd Rhode Island Artillery. Companies C and F of the 54th stayed behind to guard their camp.

The transports traveled south all night and rendezvoused the next morning with two federal gunboats. Then all four ships steamed up the Altamaha River toward Darien, Georgia, approximately ten miles inland.

Shaw was alarmed when the gunboats, at Montgomery's orders, began shelling all the houses they saw.

He could not have known, Shaw wrote later, "how many women and children might be there."

That was just the beginning of the painful ordeal for the men and officers of the 54th. The town, which sat on high sandy bluffs overlooking the river, had 75 to 100 homes and 3 churches on beautiful, tree-lined streets. There was also a school, courthouse, produce store, and a jail. Lining the river were several huge warehouses.

Montgomery told his men to take whatever they wanted, but Shaw gave his officers and men strict instructions to carry away only items that would be useful in camp.

When the plundering was finally over, Shaw said, Montgomery turned to him and said, " 'I shall burn this town.' He speaks in a very low tone, and has quite a sweet smile when addressing you. I told him I did not want the responsibility of it, and he was only too happy to take it all on his own shoulders. . . .

"The reasons he gave me for destroying Darien were that the Southerners must be made to feel that this was a real war, and that they were to be swept away by the hand of God like the Jews of old."

Shaw protested, but Montgomery was determined. The men gathered around Shaw quietly in the public square as the first torches were lit. Montgomery ordered one company of the 54th to help in the burning. Shaw was unable to countermand his order and the men had to obey.

They went about their work halfheartedly while their comrades and officers watched in silence. The smoke and flames rose so high they could be seen miles away at the regimental camp by Corporal Peal and the others who'd been left behind. Watching anxiously, they wondered what was happening to their friends.

Montgomery himself set fire to the last buildings. All that he spared was a black church, the cabin of a free black man, and a few small houses. Several slaves found in the town were taken onto the ships.

Suddenly a strong wind rose, and in moments a roaring wall of flame sent men scrambling down the bluffs and onto the transports. Their gun barrels became so hot the men were ordered to point them skyward, lest they go off and kill or wound those nearby.

The warehouses were now a sheet of flame that drove the men to the far side of the ships. Any change in wind and the fire would touch the boats with their loaded ammunition magazines, blowing them and the men to pieces.

The ropes were hurriedly cast off and finally the ships were able to get underway, just barely escaping destruction. The next day they reached camp where Shaw promptly wrote his wife that the raid was "as abominable a job" as he had ever taken part in and worried that it would "harm very much the reputation of black troops and those connected with them."

Reaction in the North was stunned disbelief. A friend of Shaw's summed up the anger and embarrassment felt by friends of the 54th when he wrote the War Department that the raid was "burning and pillaging . . . it is not war, it is piracy. . . ."

Lincoln, already displeased with Hunter, soon fired him. The 54th went on no more raids with Montgomery. Instead, they were soon moved across the harbor to St. Helena Island where many white regiments were preparing for an attack against the fortifications guarding Charleston Harbor.

On the short night journey, Montgomery shot and wounded one of his soldiers for talking after an order had been given for silence. By now Shaw was so used to Montgomery's violence that the only thing that surprised him was Montgomery's bad aim. He told Shaw he'd wanted to kill the man and toss his body into the sea.

At first it seemed the 54th would not be part of the attack. The regiment was assigned to fatigue duty, the heavy labor of digging trenches and preparing fortifications. All troops were required to do some of this, but many commanders said they would use black soldiers only for fatigue duty and not for combat.

Governor Andrew and Shaw were both afraid this might happen, and Andrew had written to Secretary Stanton a few weeks before, stressing that the regiment had been "raised and officered for *active*, not for *fatigue* duty."

But now the men of the 54th found themselves treated more like uniformed laborers than U.S. soldiers.

The black troops of Montgomery's command were frequently used not only for fatigue, but as cleaning men in the quarters of the white troops. When several men from the 54th refused an order from Montgomery's officers to perform similar duty, they were placed under arrest. The rest of the regiment threatened to take action, and those arrested were quickly released.

"It has come to the knowledge of the Brig. Gen. Commanding that detachments of colored troops, detailed for fatigue duty, have been employed in one instance at least, to prepare camps and perform menial duty for white troops," wrote an official of the adjutant general's office. "Such use of these details is unauthorized and improper, and is hereafter expressly prohibited."

Company C's William Kelly, a 19-year-old from New Bedford, went to a local barber shop one day for a shave. The barbers were black, but their customers were white. So, like the white barbers on the island, they refused to accept black customers and turned away Corporal Kelly.

Kelly returned in the evening with several of his New Bedford friends, as the barbers sat in their chairs listening to a band concert.

Kelly and his friends surrounded the shop, which sat up on wooden posts several feet above the sand. As the "last strains of music were being delivered, one side of the barber shop was lifted high and then suddenly dropped; it came down with a crash making a wreck of the building and its contents, except the barbers, who escaped unhurt, but who never made their appearance again. The episode resulted in the issuing of an order forbidding discrimination."

On June 30, the regiment was mustered for pay

for the first time. There the men and officers learned that the black troops would not receive equal pay with whites. Instead of receiving $13 a month plus a clothing allowance like the whites, they would be paid the $10 a month rate given laborers, minus $3 for clothing.

This was a blow both to the pride of the soldiers and to their ability to care for their families. Many had joined up only after being convinced they would be financially able to provide for the loved ones they'd left behind.

The men were furious and refused to accept the reduced pay. They had enlisted, Shaw said indignantly, "on the express understanding that they were to be on precisely the same footing as all other Massachusetts troops."

Since they were now being treated unequally, Shaw wrote Andrew two days after the incident, "in my opinion they should be mustered out of the service or receive the full pay which was promised them. If he [the paymaster] does not change his mind, I shall refuse to have the regiment paid until I hear from you. . . .

"Another change that has been spoken of was the arming of negro troops with pikes instead of firearms. Whoever proposed it must have been looking for a means of annihilating negro troops altogether. . . . The project is now abandoned, I believe."

Andrew replied that there had been some mistake and that "the Secretary of War will cause right to be done as soon as the case is presented to him and shall be fully understood."

Right was not done by the secretary, however, and for a year and a half the men refused to accept their pay, until Congress made it equal with that of whites.

One soldier, telling of the hardship the black troops faced, wrote: "Our families at home are in a suffering condition, and send to their husbands for relief. Where is it to come from? . . . My wife and three little children at home are, in a manner . . . starving to death. She writes to me for aid, but I have nothing to send her. . . ."

But despite the government's treatment of them, the men were still eager to go into battle.

The white regiments began leaving the island to prepare for an assault on the fortifications protecting Charleston, and by July 3 most of them were gone. The men of the 54th were bitterly disappointed at being left behind and feared the army would never use them as anything but laborers.

When the 54th was on St. Helena, the island was the site of an experiment designed to prove that ex-slaves were as capable of learning as whites. The Port Royal Experiment was sponsored by the U.S. government and supervised by the army, but Northern abolitionists supplied the teachers and money necessary to provide schooling for several thousand men, women, and children.

The ex-slaves were also given small plots of land

on plantations the government seized from Confederate slaveowners. This part of the experiment was meant to prove to those who feared free blacks would be a burden on society, that they could be self-sufficient if given the opportunity.

The slaves had been treated in ways that few free men could imagine. One day while out riding on St. Simons Island, before coming to St. Helena's, Shaw came upon several ex-slaves living in an abandoned plantation house and they told him about the "weeping day" four years before. On that day 436 men, women, and children had been auctioned off to "bearish and profane" slave speculators from Georgia, the Carolinas, Alabama, and Louisiana.

Whole families had been broken up, with mothers clinging desperately to their children. Fathers, mothers, daughters, and sons were all torn from each other and taken off in chains, never to be seen again by those they loved.

The people in the house asked Shaw if he could bring back the children. He rode away saddened by their pain, but confident that those freed from slavery could now build new lives on the abandoned plantations.

One of the first teachers to volunteer for the experiment on St. Helena was Charlotte Forten, who believed, like most of the teachers, that the future of black Americans would be largely determined by the success or failure of this experiment in self-sufficiency and education. In their minds, the experi-

ment would go hand-in-hand with the hoped-for
battlefield valor of black soldiers to guarantee racial
equality.

Charlotte was the granddaughter of James Forten,
Sr., an inventor, veteran of the Revolutionary War,
and one of this country's first black abolitionists.
Shortly after the Revolution, he was one of several
free black signers of a petition calling for modifica-
tion of the Fugitive Slave Act passed during George
Washington's second term. These signers also asked
for an end to the slave trade.

Congress overwhelmingly rejected the petition,
leading Forten to dedicate the rest of his life to fighting slavery. It was an example that greatly influenced
his granddaughter's life and her decision to go to St.
Helena.

On July 2, Colonel Shaw rode to a Baptist church
where some of the classes were held and had tea with
Charlotte and other teachers. The two had much to
talk about, for she had taught school near Boston
and they knew some of the same people.

"I am perfectly charmed with Col. Shaw," she
wrote in her diary that night. ". . . We had a very
pleasant talk on the moonlit piazza, and then went
to the Praise House to see the shout. . . . The Col.
looked and listened with the deepest interest, and
after it was over, expressed himself much gratified.
He said, he w'ld like to have some of the hymns to
send home. I shall be only too glad to copy them
for him."

On July 6, Charlotte accepted an invitation from the officers of the 54th to have tea with them at their camp. Though she was tired, she rode over on her horse.

"We were just in time to see the Dress Parade," she wrote the next day. "'Tis a splendid looking reg [regiment] — an honor to the race. Then we went with Col. Shaw to tea. Afterward sat outside the tent, and listened to some very fine singing from some of the privates. Their voices blended beautifully."

Charlotte said there was a rising moon as she left and "the low, musical murmur of the waves" washing the shore. Shaw and his men, she noted, "are eager to be called into active service."

Even as she and Shaw spoke in a countryside filled with "a deep peace," the call was on its way.

A few hours earlier the colonel had written to General George Strong, Hunter's successor, expressing his disappointment "that my regiment no longer forms a part of the force under your command. I was the more disappointed at being left behind, that I had been given to understand that we were to have our share in the work in this department. . . .

"It seems to me quite important that the colored soldiers should be associated as much as possible with white troops, in order that they may have other witnesses besides their own officers to what they are capable of doing. . . ."

Two days later the 54th received orders at noon

to be ready to move at an hour's notice, carrying only rations and blankets. One hundred men were to stay behind to guard the camp. At 3 P.M. the men began to embark on two small steamers, the *Cossack* and the *Chasseur*, and by late afternoon were sailing north toward Charleston.

Fittingly enough, thunder and lightning roared and flashed around them as the ships pulled out to sea, as if warning them of a greater storm to come.

5

"Praise from
a Thousand Homes"

Charleston was the heart of the Confederacy. Before the war was seven months old, President Lincoln ordered Union forces to try and capture the city. All attempts had failed, however, and it was still in Confederate hands.

Fort Sumter, in the middle of Charleston Harbor, guarded the city, and was in turn guarded by Fort Wagner 2,600 yards away, where the harbor met the Atlantic Ocean. No one could take Charleston without first taking Wagner.

The Union military forces were now in a better position to attack Charleston than ever before, thanks to information brought them by Robert Smalls. Smalls was a slave who piloted a 140-foot ship called *Planter*, which was so large it could hold 1,000 soldiers.

On the night of May 13, 1862, Smalls loaded his

own and several other families onto the ship, then piloted it past the guns of Fort Sumter and into the hands of the blockading Union fleet.

"I thought it might be of some service to Uncle Abe," Smalls said. The information he brought was so valuable, General Hunter sent him to Washington to talk to President Lincoln and Secretary Stanton.

The capture of Charleston was especially important to the men of the 54th, for it was the stronghold of slavery. Uncounted thousands had been sold into lives of endless toil from its slave pens. Even now, as the Union ships steamed through the night, the pens held terrified men, women, and children waiting to be placed on the auction block.

These were the people the men had vowed to save or die trying to save.

The *Chasseur* and *Cossack* rolled and battered their way north through stormy seas. The men in their rain-soaked clothes, jammed into small passageways and holds, had little food and water. The heat was stiffling, and many of the men were sick as the sea rolled the ship now this way, now that way.

The next morning the two ships made their way up the Stono River just south of the harbor. They were accompanied by four warships and eleven troop ships. All were part of a force intended to divert the Confederates from an even larger force whose object was to capture Morris Island, with Fort Wagner at the far end.

For the next three days the men of the 54th were kept onboard the *Chasseur* while the sound of battle came from Morris. At sunset on the tenth their spirits lifted when they received word the Union Army now held all the island south of Wagner, but the next morning brought bitter news: the attack against Wagner itself had failed.

The 54th now landed on James Island adjacent to Morris, and set up camp in the ditches and trenches of a field, trying to escape the glaring sun. Like all the other troops, they still had almost no food or water.

The men went out on picket duty in front of the main force, so they could watch the enemy's movements and warn of any attack. This was the first time they'd served with white troops and Shaw wrote that his men "had no trouble with them."

Sometimes they were in sight of the Confederate pickets, who gave the men "three days to clear out." For four days, though, they saw few Rebel soldiers. Then suddenly all that changed.

It was July 15, and four companies of the 54th were on picket duty about 6 P.M. under Captain Simpkins. To the left of them, also on picket duty, were soldiers of the 10th Connecticut [white] Regiment. Behind the 10th was a swamp, and to their left the river, which meant they had no way to retreat if Confederates broke through the line held by the 54th.

It began to rain and grow steadily darker. Shots

rang out, but the men could see nothing. Captain
Willard Howard of Company I climbed to the roof
of a deserted house and saw Confederates signaling
to each other. He quickly passed word to other officers to prepare for an attack.

The night passed slowly, with shadowy figures hurriedly appearing and disappearing in front of the line.
Private George Brown of Company B, whose sergeant called him a "dare-devil fellow," crawled on
his hands and knees and shot at the Confederate
pickets. Then the satisfied 20-year-old Pennsylvania
farmer crawled safely back to his comrades.

The attack came at dawn, July 16, and it came
right at the 54th.

The Confederates fired heavy field guns at the
same time the pickets were attacked. It took just
seconds for the main body of the 54th to form a
battle line, with Shaw facing the line toward the
sound of the firing. In front and out of sight of the
main body, the pickets were already fighting.

It was still dark, but the men in the rear could
hear the sound of commands and men marching toward them. Shaw held them ready.

Then five regiments of Rebels came out of the
gloom, yelling shrilly as they hurled themselves at
the 54th.

They came so fast, said First Sergeant Peter Vogelsang, that one second he was waiting for the attack to begin and the next "one hundred Rebels were
swarming about me."

Vogelsang led his men toward the left where other members of the 54th were fighting, firing steadily as the bullets crashed around them. On the way he stopped to take a musket from a dead Rebel.

"The bullets whistled so close that I could feel the wind of them," Segeant Robert Simmons of Company B wrote his mother in New York City.

A Confederate cavalryman charged Company H's Captain Cabot J. Russel, swinging his sword at Russel's head and missing. As the sword swept down a second time, Private Preston Williams of Galesburg, Illinois, blocked it with his gun and shot the Rebel through the neck.

Sergeant Joseph D. Wilson of Company H, known as the best-looking man in the regiment, had always said he would never retreat. When the attack came he ordered his men to stand and fight. Five Confederates, hearing him yelling orders, charged him and he quickly killed or wounded three of them. The others fled.

Then several Confederate cavalrymen raced toward him. Though he hadn't had time to reload his musket, Wilson leaped at them with his bayonet, fighting furiously. At last, with his body fatally ripped by bullets, Wilson fell.

The men of the 54th gave way slowly, contesting every inch of ground. "Our men fought like tigers," one of the sergeants declared.

Some were driven into the river and drowned, but most fell back fighting step by step till they reached the main body of troops. Many of the pickets were wounded.

One soldier, his right arm shattered, clung to his musket with his left hand. Captain Russel, a slightly built 19-year-old from New York City, came staggering in supporting a soldier much bigger than himself.

Captain Simpkins had bullet holes all through his pants and coat, but was untouched himself.

As the pickets reached the rest of their regiment, they fell into line and prepared to meet the enemy's charge.

While the fighting was going on, the men of the 10th Connecticut used the time given them by the 54th's fierce resistance to escape the deathtrap beside the swamp. They were just in time. Another five minutes, said one officer, and they would have been trapped.

The Confederates advanced to within about 600 yards of the Union lines, and began firing artillery. The Union soldiers stood anxiously waiting for the attack while shells and bullets screamed overhead, cutting the branches from trees.

In the front of the line, at its most vital part, stood the 54th. Then the soldiers heard a sound they had long awaited.

"Every ear was strained to catch the welcome sound," said one officer, "and at last it came in great booms. . . ."

It was the sound of the firing of the big guns on

the Union ships *John Adams* and the *Mayflower*. During the night they had steamed up the river to support the troops.

The Rebels quickly retreated, and two companies of the 54th advanced. They were followed by the rest of the regiment, which soon took up the positions they had held before the attack.

Along the way they found a trail of equipment and guns thrown away by the retreating Confederates. They also found many dead and wounded. One was a boy in a Confederate uniform, "almost a child, with soft skin and long fair hair."

They buried him "tenderly."

And then they found their own dead and wounded. Some of the wounded, who'd hidden themselves in the brush, said that captured 54th soldiers had been protected whenever there were Confederate officers present. But where there weren't any officers, the soldiers said, their comrades had been bayoneted and shot.

The official report of the regiment put the battle's cost in stark, unemotional terms: "Companies B, H and K driven in while on picket duty on the morning of July 16th, 1863. Loss in the several companies –x– Total out of less than 200 engaged, 14 killed, 17 wounded and 13 missing."

Most of the missing would never be seen again. One of those who died was Corporal Henry Dennis, a laborer from Ithaca, New York, who drowned after being forced into the river.

Also killed was Corporal Charles M. Holloway, a 24-year-old student from Wilberforce, Ohio, who was one of the last men to join the regiment. Holloway arrived at Camp Meigs on May 12, and so had been in the army just a little over two months when he died.

Private Caldwell, Sojourner Truth's grandson, was one of the missing.

For the first time the 54th had been bloodied. For the first time its ranks had been depleted by battle. For the first time it knew the sorrow of burying friends and comrades. And now on these islands within a stone's throw of the heart of the Confederacy, the men of the 54th also knew that if their bravery could help bring freedom to those still enslaved, then freedom would soon come to millions in chains.

Others knew it, too, and others acknowledged their courage.

"But for the bravery of three companies of the Massachusetts Fifty-fourth (colored), our whole regiment would have been captured," one member of the 10th Connecticut wrote his mother. "As it was, we had to double-quick in, to avoid being cut off by the rebel cavalry. They fought like heroes."

"They showed no sign of fear but fought as if they were very angry and determined to have revenge," said a Boston reporter. "Had the 54th given way, the retreat of the 10th would have been cut off, and they would have been absolutely annihilated or captured."

"The boys of the Tenth Connecticut could not help loving the men who saved them from destruction," reported another newspaper correspondent from the scene of battle. "I have been deeply affected at hearing this feeling expressed by officers and men of the Connecticut regiment; and probably a thousand homes from Windham to Fairfield have, in letters, been told the story of how the dark-skinned heroes fought the good fight and covered with their own brave hearts the retreat of brothers, sons, and fathers of Connecticut."

General Alfred H. Terry, who was in charge of the diversionary attack on James Island, told one of Shaw's officers to inform the colonel that he was "exceedingly pleased with the conduct of your regiment."

That evening Shaw wrote proudly to his wife Annie: "All this is very gratifying to us personally, and a fine thing for our coloured troops."

That night the 54th was ordered to evacuate James, along with the rest of the troops. Their maneuver had been successful and had enabled the Union forces to capture most of Morris Island.

The Union regiments began to move to the other side of James that night, with the 54th leading the way. Again rain pelted their faces and soaked their weary bodies at the beginning of their journey. Again the thunder and the lightning flashed. Again they headed off to battle without complaining.

But surely, as they struggled through the darkness,

some must have wondered how much more pain and sorrow they and their comrades would have to endure before their quest was over.

William C. Nell, a black abolitionist who once helped lead the fight against the Fugitive Slave Act of 1850, had watched the 54th march through Boston on the day of their departure.

Nell, who was also an historian, declared in awe: "Glory enough for one day; aye, indeed, for a lifetime."

Would the battle they were about to fight bring them glory enough for one day? Or, indeed, for a lifetime?

Soon the men of the 54th, pilgrims journeying under yet another starless sky, would know the answer.

6
"Tonight We'll Sleep in Wagner"

Shaw led the way, accompanied by engineers who knew the terrain. The march was like a nightmare for the tired and hungry soldiers.

Lewis Douglass later wrote his father: "That night we took, according to one of our officers, one of the hardest marches on record, through woods and marsh."

A strong wind constantly drove the rain against their faces, and the path grew steadily narrower. At first two men could walk abreast, then the path was barely wide enough for one.

The only light was from lightning flashes, and each man had to hold onto the man in front of him as they inched their way across swaying planks spanning long stretches of deep water. The rickety little bridges had no handrails and soon became slippery with mud.

Often the men fell in, and had to struggle furiously to raise themselves back onto the planks. Soon their clothes and bodies were soaked with stagnant swamp water.

All night thunder sounded like a mournful drum, and the quick flashes of lightning left them groping in darkness that seemed even blacker than before.

The ground was soaked and the soles of their boots were soon covered with big lumps of clay. When they left a swamp and entered woods, the branches slapped at their hands and faces until they were cov-ered with cuts.

The men had started at 10 P.M. Seven hours later they had covered only four miles. At last, as dawn came and the rain stopped, the first of the men reached solid ground. They flung themselves down and immediately fell asleep, while the rest of the regiment gradually made its way through the last of the swamps.

When all the men were there, they marched to the beach on the ocean side of the island. Across the water was Folly Island, a narrow strip of land that ran almost all the way to Morris Island. Folly was to be the jumping off point for the attack on Wagner, and regiments arrived and departed all morning. The men of the 54th, though, spent the day on the furnace-like white sand of the beach.

At first they slept, but as the sun rose higher sleep

became impossible. There was no food except for a few crackers, and huge crowds of soldiers gathered around the few sources of water. All of the men, including the officers, still wore the same clothes they'd worn when they left St. Helena eight days before.

Many of the men closed their eyes to try and shut out the glare, but there was no escaping the heat. They were close to exhaustion.

The hours passed slowly. It was July 17. Unknown to the men of the 54th, anti-black riots had raged throughout the North while they were fighting on James Island the day before.

In March, the Congress had passed the first draft law in the nation's history. It allowed a man to escape army duty if he paid the government $300. On Sunday, July 12, the names of the first men to be drafted were printed in the newspapers. Many of them were Irish immigrants.

The next morning mobs in New York City, outraged at the idea of having to risk their lives to end slavery and fearful that the freed slaves would come North and take their jobs, began attacking every black person they saw. The rioters were encouraged by politicians, newspaper editors, and businessmen with investments in the South, who opposed Lincoln's emancipation policy. At first the rioters yelled "Down with rich men," "Down with police," and "Down with the draft." But soon all their fury was directed against black men, women, and children.

The reign of terror roared out of control from July 13 through July 16, with black people being hunted down and chased like "hounds would chase a fox," one United States official said in an urgent telegram to Secretary Stanton.

Many blacks ran to the waterfront and hid under piers, or were driven into the water and drowned. Some sought refuge in police stations, but the police could barely protect themselves. Others hid in barns on Long Island or fled to Blackwell's Island in the East River where they cowered in woods. Still others tried to lose themselves in swamps across the Hudson River in New Jersey.

A mob that included many women and children broke into the Colored Orphan Asylum on Fifth Avenue and began destroying everything they could as the 233 children were hurried out the back door by the director. The screaming mob looted the orphanage, even taking the children's clothes. Then, still howling its hate, the mob tried to set fire to the four-story building.

Twice they tried and twice ten firemen, under Chief John Decker, quickly doused the flames. But soon smoke and fire poured from every part of the orphanage and within hours, said one observer, hardly a brick was left standing.

Some of the children were taken to the arsenal at Thirty-fourth Street for protection, while others were taken to the Thirty-fourth Street police station.

The building housing Horace Greeley's *New York*

Tribune, one of President Lincoln's biggest support-ers, was almost destroyed. The rioters also came to the block where Sergeant Robert Simmons' mother, sister, and his sister's two children lived. Too late his sister decided to try and take the children, one a baby, and the other a physically handicapped seven-year-old boy, to a safer part of the city.

The rioters descended on her son, who could not keep up with her. She turned and started back as the mob surrounded him, beating him with sticks and hitting him with heavy paving stones torn from the street. One man ran up and smashed the boy across the temple with the butt of a pistol.

His mother was unable to reach him, but a fireman named John McGovern charged through the mob, grabbed the child, and took him to the home of a German immigrant family who nursed him "with more than a mother's care."

Sergeant Simmons' sister, when she finally found her son, knelt by his bedside and thanked God for saving him, but the child soon died. The mob also burned down their house.

The fury of the frenzied mobs spread like a hur-ricane and soon they were attacking the homes of leading abolitionists.

Shaw's father lived on Staten Island, and it was rumored that mobs were coming to burn his house. While Colonel Shaw led the 54th through the swamps on James Island, his father quickly sent away his wife and daughters and stayed on with his son-in-law to protect the house. The mob never came, however.

Union Army troops were rushed to New York from the Battle of Gettysburg to restore order.

In New Bedford, Massachusetts, home of Sergeant William Carney and 30 other members of Company C, mobs broke into the Colored Sailors Home and terrorized the manager and his family. Finally they managed to escape to the roof of a nearby house.

All the while, said William Powell, the manager, the rain poured down "as if the very heavens were shedding tears over the dreadful calamity.

"How to escape from the roof of a five-story building with four females — and one a cripple — without a ladder was beyond my *not* excited imagination," he wrote a friend.

"But God came to my relief in the person of a little deformed Israelite who took my poor helpless daughter under his protection in his house. He also supplied me with a long rope. . . . I managed to lower my family down to the next roof and from one roof to another, until I landed them in a neighbor's yard."

Powell then took his family to the police station for safety and found "upward of seventy men, women, and children — some with broken limbs — bruised and beaten from head to foot. We stayed in this place for 24 hours, when the police escorted us to the New Haven boat. . . . I am now an old man, stripped of everything which I once possessed, but I thank God that He has spared my life which

I am ready to yield in the defense of my country."

The riot in New York City is still classified as the deadliest riot this country has ever seen. Scores of victims were hung from lampposts and trees, and black homes throughout the city were burned to the ground.

Three days later the children from the orphanage, whose ages ranged from two years old to fifteen, were marched to the North River under armed guard. They were followed by black adults carrying small bundles of clothing and the few small objects they had been able to save from their ruined homes.

Surrounded by 40 policemen and over 100 soldiers, they began boarding ships that would take them to safety.

While the men, women, and children were still boarding, a menacing crowd gathered. The colonel in charge ordered his men to face the mob with fixed bayonets, which they did, holding them in check until all the ships were safely away from the pier.

Almost 1,000 miles to the south, Sergeant Simmons sat on the beach and wrote his mother:

"We fought a desperate battle. . . . God has protected me through this, my first fiery leaden trial, and I do give him the glory, and render praises unto His holy name. . . . God bless you all! Goodbye! Likely we shall be engaged again soon. Your affectionate son, R.J. Simmons."

At last dusk came and with it the ship that would take the men over to Folly Island. All the other

regiments had already left. There was no pier for the
ship to tie up to, however, and the men had to be
rowed out in a leaky longboat that held about 30 at
a time. It was 10 P.M. before the first men left,
laboriously making their way into the boat by the
light of a single lantern.

The thunder came again, and again the rain drove
into their faces.

Each trip seemed to take forever, with the rowers
constantly fighting a strong current and the boat so
crowded the rowers barely had room to move their
arms.

The men left on the beach stood in clothes long
since soaked, and with boots that oozed water. Rain
ran down their faces in small torrents.

Though he had been offered a cabin on the
steamer, Shaw stayed with them. It was daylight
before he stepped in with the last boat load and was
taken to the ship.

He stood on the deck talking with Hallowell, then
he disappeared. Hallowell went looking for him and
found him lying near the pilot's house on the top
deck.

"Oh Ned!" Shaw said. "If I could live a few
weeks longer with my wife, and be home a little
while I think I might die happy. But it cannot be.
I do not believe I will live through our next
fight."

Then Shaw asked to be left alone. An hour later
he came up to Hallowell.

Governor John Andrew of Massachusetts petitioned the government to recruit black troops for the war.

Frederick Douglass, leading abolitionist, journalist, and recruiter for the Massachusetts 54th, is pictured here with his grandson.

Colonel Robert Gould Shaw, commanding officer of the Massachusetts 54th Regiment.

Martin R. Delaney, a physician by occupation, became the first black field officer in the Union Army.

COME AND JOIN US BROTHERS.

A Civil War recruitment poster calling for black troops.

A Frank Leslie illustration of a New York City recruitment office.

The Colored Orphan Asylum, housing over 200 children, was set afire in the wake of the New York City draft riots.

Second Lt. Stephen A. Swails of Company F, who served at Fort Wagner.

Second Lt. Peter Vogelsang of Company H, another black officer who fought at Fort Wagner.

Sgt. William H. Carney received the Congressional Medal of Honor for his valiant effort at Fort Wagner, where he carried the flag across Union lines declaring, "The old flag never touched the ground."

Charlotte Forten was a teacher from Massachusetts who established a school in South Carolina for the children of ex-slaves.

Robert Smalls was hailed as a hero by Yankee newspapers when he steered the confederate gunboat the *Planter* across Union lines.

Men of the 1st New York Engineers and members of the Massachusetts 54th worked together to build barriers against rebel fire at Wagner.

Members of the Massachusetts 54th Regiment stand alongside a bombproof shelter at Fort Wagner.

Victorious black troops parade through the streets of Charleston at the end of the war.

The Shaw Memorial at the Boston Common. Erected in 1897, it was the first monument honoring a regiment.

"All sadness had passed from his face, and he was perfectly cheerful . . .," Hallowell remembered.

By 9 A.M. the steamer had taken them as far up the island as it could go, and the regiment disembarked. They then had to march six miles to Lighthouse Inlet, a narrow body of water that separated Folly from Morris.

As they marched, white soldiers in camps along the route called out words of praise for their bravery two days before.

"Hurrah, boys! you saved the Tenth Connecticut!" some cried. "Well done! we heard your guns!" yelled others.

One group of soldiers found a box of hard, water-soaked bread and quickly ate it.

The regiment finally left the woods and marched along the beach where the going was easier. Squalls of rain fell intermittently. A newspaper correspondent covering the attack later told Governor Andrew, "I saw them and they looked worn and weary."

As they marched, the soldiers could hear the steady sound of artillery fire. Reaching Lighthouse Inlet, many of the men formed a circle around the regimental flags planted in the sand and began singing. Their deep voices carried through the hot summer air in song after song. Then finally, as the day wore on and the time for battle drew near, they closed with a song so mournful some generals refused to allow their troops to sing it: "When This Cruel War Is Over."

"It was the last song of many," said one officer, "but few then thought it a requiem":

". . . If amid the din of battle Nobly you
    should fall,
Far away from those that love you, None
    to hear your call.
Who would whisper words of comfort,
    Who would soothe your pain?
Ah! the many cruel fantasies Ever in my
    brain. . . .

"Weeping, sad and lonely, Hopes and
    fears how vain!
When this cruel war is over, Praying that
    we meet again!"

The last strains died away and the men prepared to leave. All afternoon the cannons had roared as 11 Union warships pounded Fort Wagner. The *New Ironsides*, a three-decked armorclad ship carrying the heaviest cannon ever floated, hurled 150-pound shells at Wagner for almost four hours.

The warships were joined by heavy Union batteries set up on Morris within the last week. Shells burst in the fort and in the air, while others bounded over the sand into the fort. Soon the island around Wagner was a smoking inferno.

"Nothing like the rapid discharge from heavy artillery has ever been seen or heard before on this continent," declared the *Richmond Examiner*.

A chaplain from one of the Union regiments watched the bombardment and wrote: "Words cannot depict the thunder, the smoke, the lifted sand and the general havoc which characterized that hot summer day. What a storm of iron fell on that island; the roar of the guns was incessant; how the shots ploughed the sand banks and the marshes; how the splinters flew from the Beacon House; how the whole island smoked like a furnace and trembled as from an earthquake."

General W.B. Taliaferro, the Confederate commander at Wagner, estimated that "not less than 9,000 solid shot and shell were thrown in against the battery during the eleven hours the bombardment lasted."

Union commanders, gathered on Morris Island's highest sandhill within sight of Charleston, thought Wagner was crippled.

At about 4 p.m., the occasional return fire from Wagner totally ceased, and not a single Confederate soldier could be seen on the walls.

The belief was widespread, said one officer of the 54th, "that the enemy had been driven from his shelter, and the armament of Wagner rendered harmless."

Inside the fort, though, General Taliaferro had carefully prepared for the anticipated assault. He ordered his men to surround all but a handful of the

lighter guns with sandbags and to bury the heavy
field guns totally in sand. Then he ordered all but a
few gunners to take shelter in the bombproofs, which
could hold almost 1,800 men, and stay there until
the firing ceased.

As a result, when the bombardment ended, all the
big guns were still intact and only eight men out of
almost 1,700 in the fort had been killed. The rest
waited for the attack.

General Truman Seymour, the Union commander
of the assault, gathered his officers around him.
Colonel H.S. Putnam of New Hampshire bitterly
protested the decision to storm the fort saying: "We
are going into Wagner like a flock of sheep."

But Seymour was confident and couldn't be
stopped. "I can run right over it," he said. "I can
camp my whole command there in one night." He
decided to attack at twilight.

It was late afternoon and time for the men to cross
over to Morris. Once they landed, they stayed near
the shore, waiting for further orders.

Shaw reported to the headquarters of General
George C. Strong, commander of the brigade that
included the 54th and five other regiments. (There
were three brigades in all.)

"You may lead the column, if you say yes," the
general told Shaw. "Your men, I know, are worn
out, but do as you choose." The battle lines were
already forming.

Shaw's face brightened and he had his men

brought up. Most of the other regiments were already in place for the attack. The regiment marched out as the rest of the army watched, regimental flags flying in a gentle breeze.

Shaw marched the regiment near the sea, where they formed two lines, the men on the right standing almost in the ocean. The officers ordered them to lie down with their bayonets fixed, until the regiments behind could finish forming into attacking columns.

It was 6 P.M.

A cannonball passed close overhead, and one man moved nervously. Hallowell quickly told the man to be quiet.

"I guess the major forgets what kind of balls those are!" one of the soldiers said, laughing.

Strong rode up and spoke briefly to the men. "I am sorry you must go into the fight tired and hungry," he told them, "but the men in the fort are tired too. There are but three hundred behind those walls and they have been fighting all day. Don't fire a musket on the way up, but go in and bayonet them at their guns."

Then he pointed to Oberlin's John Wall, bearing the Stars and Stripes and said, "If this man should fall, who will lift the flag and carry it on?"

Shaw, standing beside Strong, took his cigar from his mouth and said quietly but clearly, "I will."

The men cheered wildly. Shaw listened for a few moments and then said: "I want you to prove yourselves. The eyes of thousands will look on what you do tonight."

He was calm, but noticing a slight twitching at the corners of his mouth, one of the officers said he knew Shaw had counted "the whole cost" of the sacrifice about to be made.

Earlier Shaw had decided he would lead the right column or wing (Companies K, C, I, A, and B), and Hallowell the left (Companies H, F, G, D, and E).

As they stood waiting for the sun to set, Shaw sent his horse back with a request for Charlotte Forten to take care of it until his return, or send it home to Annie if he failed to return.

It was now almost 6:30 P.M.

To the east a fog gathered over the sea; to the west the sun was setting but the sky still burned bright. A shell passed overhead; another fell into the sea.

Once in awhile a lone horseman rode to the regiments in the rear with orders, the hoofbeats stark and lonely in the eerie silence of thousands of quietly watching men.

At last the regiments behind were almost ready. The 6th Connecticut took up position directly behind the 54th, and the other 12 regiments lined up behind the 6th.

The twilight deepened. Time seemed to stand still.

At last Shaw walked to the front of the regiment. "Attention!" he called.

Men sprang to their feet, whispering last-minute advice to each other even as they listened to their colonel. The officers felt their pistols and grasped each other's hands.

Shaw told the men to make sure their bayonets were securely fastened. Then, after a brief pause, he gave the order: "Move in quick time until within a hundred yards of the fort, then double quick and charge!" Then, after another slight pause, he gave the final command: "Forward!"

It was, said one man, "a beautiful and calm evening."

The regiment, reduced to a little over 600 men and 19 officers by the losses at James Island and details left behind for fatigue and guard duty, began to move.

To their right was the ocean at high tide, to their left a marsh two miles wide. Some men already struggled in knee-deep water. The sand ahead narrowed steadily as it neared the fort.

They heard the artillery mixed with their own labored breathing, waves washing the shore, and the tramp of hundreds of feet on sand.

The fort stood before them like a dark and silent tomb.

One of the soldiers looked at it and said, "Tonight we'll sleep in Wagner."

7
"One Gallant Rush"

It was 7:45 when the 54th began its charge. The sky was almost dark, and the massive fort loomed three quarters of a mile away.

The guns of Wagner fell silent as Shaw led the men, sword upraised and a white sash tied round his waist. His eyes, said a fellow officer, strained into the darkness.

Union artillery guns fired over the heads of the men into the fort, and from the sea came a constant pounding of Wagner even while the men charged. From Fort Sumter, Fort Gregg, and James Island, the Confederates raked the regiment with artillery fire. But Wagner was silent.

Wagner has been called the greatest earthworks ever built. Its double walls were huge. They were made of sand, earth-covered grass to hold the sand in place, and the logs of palmetto trees. Even direct hits seemed to have little effect on the giant structure.

It was armed with 16 big guns, including one with a barrel that weighed almost 8 tons and could hurl a 128-pound shell more than a mile.

Inside the fort there were the almost 1,700 men waiting with hand grenades, wooden spikes, and rifles that fired screaming metal "minié balls" with a noise like "the wailing sound of the winter's wind."

Despite all this, and the craters that dotted the way forward as a result of the Union bombardment, one officer said there was "no provision for cutting away obstructions, filling the ditch, or spiking the guns. No special instructions were given the stormers; no line of skirmishers or covering party was thrown out; no engineers or guides accompanied the column; no artillery-men to serve the captured guns; no plan of the work was shown company officers. It was understood that the fort would be assaulted with the bayonet. . . ."

The men charged steadily at quick time, which was almost two steps every second.

"Not a glimmer of light was seen," one reporter said. "Not a gun replied to the bombs which our mortars . . . hurled into the fort. Not a shot was returned to the terrific volleys of the giant frigate *Ironsides*, whose shells, ever and anon, plunged into the earthworks, illuminating their recesses for an instant in the glare of their explosion, but revealing no signs of life."

And then the Union guns ceased and all grew silent. For a moment.

Two hundred yards from the fort the island narrowed steadily. There had barely been room enough for the two lines of men when they began and now the solid ground on which they charged grew ever smaller.

The lines buckled as men were hemmed in on either side, with some now running in the high tide with water foaming around their legs, and others stumbling against each other. Most of the men in Companies B and E, on the far right of the two columns, struggled in the ocean. Many were forced to fall behind for lack of room, but still they followed Shaw and the gently waving flags they could now barely see.

As they reached the narrowest part of the strip, Shaw was running in the water at the edge of the beach. Now he turned left and charged toward the center of Wagner, where four large guns had opened fire on the regiment.

Sergeant Major Douglass, Corporal Peal, and others were at his shoulders.

As soon as the Union heavy guns had stopped firing, reported General Gillmore, "a compact and most destructive musketry fire was instantly delivered from the parapet by the garrison, which up to that moment had remained safely ensconced in the bomb-proof shelter. The troops went gallantly on, however. . . ."

The fire was deadly and many of the men were hit.

"I was either hit by a shell or knocked down by the concussion and received a wound in my head in falling, I cannot tell which," said Sergeant Benjamin Green of Company I. "I lost consciousness and when I recovered I found myself in the Rifle Pits. . . ."

Said one soldier: "A sheet of flame, followed by a running fire, like electric sparks, swept along the parapet."

All of the fort's guns were now firing. Men flew into the air and were thrown across the sand, blood pouring from their bodies. Some screamed and groaned; others lay in silence.

Still the men charged and still they waited for the order to fire.

"There had been no stop, pause or check at any period of the advance," said one officer, "nor was there now."

"Not a man flinched, though it was a trying time," remembered Sergeant Douglass. "A shell would explode and clear a space of twenty feet; our men would close up again."

The flash and lightning of cannon now filled the air, and hand grenades hurled down the slope exploded into the mass of men. The line buckled momentarily, then the men charged forward at double-quick time so they could close with the enemy sooner.

Shaw, holding his sword aloft and slashing the air for the men to follow, swept on. The flagbearers were close behind him.

Now the regiment came to a ditch or moat only fifty yards from the fort. It was filled with several feet of water and heavy, wooden spikes pointing at the attackers' chests.

Hundreds of Confederate guns blazed away at the moat, and there many of the men of the 54th died struggling in the water or trying to climb over the spikes. All the while fire poured ceaselessly upon them.

Shaw and the men pressed on, somehow finally clearing this last hurdle, though men died all around them.

"I saw him again, just for an instant, as he sprang into the ditch," Hallowell said. "His broken and shattered regiment were following him."

At last, legs churning, they were through the ditch and charging up the sloping parapet that led to the top of the fort.

The corners of the fort projected outward, so that the attacking men were caught in a raging storm that came at them from both sides and in front. On the sand behind and in the ditch lay a slaughterhouse of the dead and dying.

"The grape and canister, shell and minies swept us down like chaff," wrote Douglass to his father. "Still our men went on and on."

Private Edward Williams of Oberlin and a dozen other men were killed when a terrific shower of grapeshot exploded in their faces. Williams was never seen again.

And now on the parapet slope the Rebel soldiers were trying to beat them back with musket butts and bayonets, but the men of the 54th finally drove them back in vicious hand-to-hand combat.

"Upon leaving the ditch for the parapet," said Hallowell, "they obstinately contested our advance. Notwithstanding those difficulties, the men succeeded in driving the enemy from most of their guns, many following the enemy into the fort."

The men and officers of the 54th had still not fired a shot, saving their ammunition for the final charge into the heart of the fire.

Shaw turned to the figures struggling to follow him in the darkness up the last 30 feet. "Forward, my brave boys!" he called.

With an answering cheer and a shout they followed. And then they were at the top.

Rebel gunners on the wall fired straight down into their faces. Shaw leaped onto the wall and Douglass, almost at his shoulder, shouted for his comrades to follow.

"Come, boys, come!" he cried.

A flash of cannon fire showed Shaw, and from 20 to 40 of his men, fighting on the wall, flailing away at the gray shapes surrounding them.

"Rally! Rally!" Shaw urged the men. Then there was a flash and Shaw fell into the fort, shot through the heart. Twelve of his men fell almost at the same instant. Private Francis Myers of Company K, standing just beneath Shaw's upraised sword, lifted his arm to follow and in a moment it was shattered by a shell.

Not until Shaw was killed did the officers and soldiers of the 54th begin firing their weapons, but they were soon forced to fight again with bayonets, musket butts, and fists.

Those soldiers who managed to get into the fort now fought in a desperate circle around Shaw's body. At first the ferocity of their charge drove the Confederates back, but more and more Rebels attacked the hopelessly outnumbered band with guns, wooden spikes, gun rammers, musket and pistol shot, and anything they could get their hands on.

The huge cannons from Sumter, Gregg, and James Island tore into the men still struggling across the ditch and up the parapet, falling into shell holes and over the bodies of their comrades.

One officer said each shell made a "horrible" noise as if "50 Locomotive Whistles were blowing at once."

Hand grenades filled the air with flying metal fragments and explosions shook the earth. Lighted shells were dropped onto the men as they tried to climb the wall.

One grenade exploded almost on top of Douglass as he fought atop the parapet. It hurled him into the air and blew away the sword sheath wrapped around his waist. Miraculously, he was unhurt, and quickly climbed the wall to continue the fight.

Corporal Peal planted the tattered state flag at the top of the fort, so close to the enemy a Confederate soldier reached out and ripped it from the staff.

John Wall struggled just past the ditch. The Stars and Stripes he carried was also in tatters, ripped by countless shells, but still he held it high. Suddenly he was blown into the air, but before the flag could touch the earth it was grabbed by Sergeant Carney.

Carney ran up the slope and planted the flag next to the wall. While the battle raged around them, both Carney and Peal clung to the sand just outside the wall for over an hour, holding the staffs aloft.

It was hand-to-hand combat now, with men clubbing and stabbing and trying to kill each other anyway they could.

A few of the officers and men still fought inside the fort, though a fresh Confederate regiment that had just arrived from the mainland was thrown against them. Some of the soldiers who had fought their way into that part of the fort nearest the sea were trapped, but refused to surrender: "reckless and insane men," the Confederate commander called them.

The first Rebel soldiers sent to kill or capture them cowered back before the ferocity they met. Then the commander ordered the fresh troops to attack, dropping grenades and lighted shells on the men, and firing muskets and pistols.

"These troops were ordered to . . . plunge their concentrated fire over the stronghold," General Taliaferro said. "Still, for a time, the enemy held out. . . ."

"Many of the 54th men clambered over and some entered by the large embrasure in which one of the big guns was mounted," one man remembered.

Captain Appleton of Company G crawled into an embrasure [an opening in the wall where cannon were placed], and knocked out most of the gun crew with his pistol. Within moments, though, he was badly wounded.

Private George Wilson of Company A also fought at the gun and was shot through both shoulders, but refused to leave until Appleton gave his permission.

Private Daniel States of Company B was the first man to be captured. "The Confederate officer who took him from the men who secured him, placed States in the charge of several soldiers, whose names the officer took, ordering them to keep him as a prisoner-of-war, and from being killed, which some of the men in the fort wished to do," a Union officer said.

Captains Simpkins and Russel, along with Sergeant Stephen Swails of Company F, struggled up the parapet together. Russel was hit but refused to be carried off. As Swails tried to make him more comfortable, a shell hit Simpkins who "fell across Russel, and never spoke or moved again."

The men were now alone and dying fast, as they

waited in vain for the regiments to reinforce them.

"The white regiments could not be made to come up," Douglass said.

But apparently the charge of the 54th had been so quick it took everyone by surprise, including the Union commanders. By the time the supporting regiments finally moved up, the opportunity for victory was lost.

The force of the attack had broken after the initial fury, like a wave breaking on the shore. Shaw lay dead. Hallowell was wounded. Fourteen of the 54th's officers were dead or wounded, and the regiment was shattered. But still the men fought on, joined by white soldiers from New York and Connecticut. The odds were too great, though, and at last they had to retreat.

The men quickly found that going back was as deadly as coming forward had been, and again they had to run a gauntlet of fire.

"Immediately after I heard an order, 'Retreat!' some twelve or fifteen of us slid down the parapet," one man recalled. "The line of retreat seemed lit with infernal fire. The hissing bullets and bursting shells seemed angry demons."

Douglass was the last man in the regiment to leave the fort. Again the ground was filled with the dead and dying as men struggled to reach and cross the ditch. Then suddenly they were also being shot at from their own lines.

"At the very hottest moment of the struggle," said

Sergeant George Stephens of Company B, "a battalion or regiment charged up to the moat, halted, and did not attempt to cross it and join us, but from their position commenced to fire upon us. I was one of the men who shouted from where I stood, 'Don't fire on us! We are the Fifty-fourth.' I have heard it was a Maine regiment."

Confusion mounted in the darkness, filled with the screams and groans of the dying and wounded. It was enough, said Captain Luis Emilio of Company F, to make one cry out like the ancient Greek warrior Ajax, "Give us but light, O Jove! and in the light, if thou seest fit, destroy us!"

Sergeant Carney finally saw what he thought were his comrades. Raising the flag, he stood up and moved through the smoke toward them, then suddenly realized they were Rebels.

Whirling round, Carney ran for the moat, and though two shots hit him he still held the flag up high. A soldier from the 100th New York grabbed his arm and, while stumbling through the moat, Carney was wounded in the head.

Finally the New Bedford seaman staggered back to the field hospital, still carrying the flag. Some of the wounded rose from their straw mats and cheered as he collapsed beside them, saying; "The old flag never touched the ground, boys."

So many of the 54th's officers had been killed or wounded that 19-year-old Emilio, who was the ninth captain in the chain of command going into the battle, was now the senior officer.

Seven hundred yards from the fort he formed the men into an irregular line that stretched across the sand, in preparation for a second charge. An officer from another regiment ordered them to stay there and prepare instead for a Confederate counterattack, but it never came.

General Strong then led more regiments into the battle, but was killed almost immediately. Next Colonel Putnam "carried the flag of the 7th New Hampshire into the fort, which he held for half an hour without being reinforced. The enemy succeeded in bringing to bear against him ten or twelve howitzers, loaded with grape and canister, when the slaughter became so terrible that he was forced to retire, after having lost nearly all his officers."

Colonel Putnam was shot through the head and killed a short distance from the fort. Some of the men of the 54th had fought their way back into the fort with Putnam's troops, but again were forced to retreat.

The Union soldiers who made their way to the rear had one final struggle to endure before they could rest.

"Upon the beach in front of the siege line, drunken soldiers of the regular artillery, with swords and pistol shots barred the passage of all to the rear," said Emilio. "They would listen to no protestations that the regiments were driven back or broken up, and even brutally ordered wounded men to the front. After a time, their muddled senses came to them on seeing the host of arrivals, while the vigorous actions of a few determined officers who were prepared to enforce free passage, made further opposition perilous."

By midnight all firing had ceased. Shortly after 1 A.M. the 10th Connecticut relieved the men, who then marched a short distance down the beach and camped for the night in the shelter of sand bluffs.

There were less than 350 of them left. All the rest had been killed, wounded, or captured.

The bodies of their comrades and men from the other regiments stretched three quarters of a mile to Wagner, black soldiers and white soldiers who had fought and died together. The fears of those who loved them had come to pass and many now lay "on the battle plain, Lonely, wounded, even dying, Calling, but in vain."

"The battle is over; it is midnight; the ocean beach is crowded with the dead, the dying and the wounded," wrote Edward L. Pierce to Governor Andrew. Pierce, who was covering the battle for the *New York Tribune*, said, "It is with difficulty that you can urge your horse through to Lighthouse Inlet. Faint lights glimmer in the sand holes and rifle pits where many a poor bleeding soldier has lain down to his last sleep."

The men of the 54th had not captured the fort, but when their action became known it would capture a nation's heart. They had given all they had to try and free others.

"I saw them fight at Wagner as none but splendid

soldiers, splendidly officered, could fight," wrote Samuel Mason of the *New York Herald* the next day.

Months earlier Frederick Douglass, in urging them to join the regiment, had said: "The iron gate of our prison stands half open. One gallant rush . . . will fling it wide. . . ."

And so they had come to Camp Meigs, all driven by the dream of flinging wide the iron gate of slavery. And though they did not know it yet, their gallant rush that night would help four million people march out to freedom.

Again there was silence on the beach, except for the washing of the waves and the moaning of the wounded. The sky was clear and lit by stars. At last the men could rest.

8
"You Are
United States Soldiers"

The firing had barely ceased when Brigadier General Thomas G. Stevenson, commander of the front lines, ordered four companies from the 97th Pennsylvania to try and rescue the wounded lying near or within the Confederate lines.

Stevenson told them to try especially hard to find members of the 54th.

"You know how much harder they will fare at the hands of the enemy than white men," he said.

All night these white rescuers crawled along the ground, even up to the walls of the fort, listening for the moans of the wounded. Then quietly they dragged them back to their own lines. By the time the light of dawn forced a halt to their efforts, several men had been saved who would otherwise have fallen into Confederate hands.

It was, said one of the officers, "a noble work fearlessly done."

In the morning over 100 of the wounded were taken to Beaufort on the hospital ship *Cosmopolitan*. There a silent crowd of ex-slaves, many with tears in their eyes, helped carry the men on stretchers or place a helping arm around the walking wounded.

Charlotte Forten stopped her teaching when she heard the news, and hurried by rowboat from St. Helena six miles away to help tend the wounded.

"Tonight comes news, oh, so sad, so heart sickening," she wrote in her diary. "It is too terrible, too terrible to write. We can only hope it may not all be true. That our noble, beautiful young Colonel is killed, and the reg [iment] cut to pieces! I cannot, cannot believe it. And yet I know it may be so.

"But oh, I am stunned, sick at heart. I can scarcely write. There was an attack on Fort Wagner. The 54th put in advance; fought bravely, desperately, but was finally overpowered and driven back after getting into the Fort. Thank Heaven! they fought bravely! . . . . I can write no more to-night."

One of the other women who nursed the wounded men of the 54th was an ex-schoolteacher from Massachusetts named Clara Barton. Years later she would found the American Red Cross, but during the Civil War she helped set up Union hospitals and find supplies for the wounded.

General Gillmore allowed her to watch the attack from his flagship, the *Fulton*, and she never forgot it.

"I saw the bayonets glisten . . . and the dark line of blue trailed into the belching walls of Wagner," she said. "I saw them on, up, and over the parapets into the jaws of death, and heard the clang of the death-dealing sabers as they grappled with the foe. I saw . . . the wounded, slowly crawling to me down the tide-washed beach."

While the battle raged she somehow managed to get ashore, help the doctors establish a field hospital, and help the wounded. Then she went to Beaufort to nurse them further.

Years later she wrote: "I can see again the scarlet flow of blood as it rolled over the black limbs beneath my hands, and the great heave of the human heart before it grew still."

Charlotte Forten tried to mend the bullet holes and bayonet tears in the men's clothing, but sometimes "found a jacket that told a sad tale—so torn to pieces that it was far past mending."

She felt especially sad for a 19-year-old from Michigan, probably John Coleman of Company G.

"He is very badly wounded—in both legs and there is a ball—in the stomach—it is thought that it cannot be extracted," she wrote in her diary. "This poor fellow suffers terribly. His groans are pitiful to hear. But he utters no complaint, and it is touching to see his gratitude for the least kindness that one does him."

To her surprise, Private Coleman eventually recovered.

Back on the beach there was a flag of truce so the dead could be buried and the wounded taken back to their lines. The Union commanders tried in vain to find out what had happened to Shaw. So many men were missing that hope was held out he may have been captured instead of killed, but his death was soon confirmed.

"Numbers of both white and black were killed on top of our breastworks as well as inside," a Confederate lieutenant said. "The negroes fought gallantly, and were headed by as brave a colonel as ever lived. He mounted the breastworks waving his sword, and at the head of his regiment, and he and a negro orderly sergeant fell dead over the inner crest of the works. The negroes were as fine-looking a set as I ever saw—large, strong, muscular fellows."

The sergeant was apparently First Sergeant Andrew Benton of Company A, a 28-year-old waiter from Catskill, New York. Benton was reported missing after the battle, as were 99 other members of the 54th. Like many of them, he was never seen again.

Assistant Surgeon John Luck, who was taken prisoner while helping the Union wounded, said that while "being conducted into the fort, I saw Colonel Shaw . . . lying dead upon the ground just outside the parapet. A stalwart negro man had fallen near him. The Rebels said the negro was a color sergeant. The colonel had been killed by a rifle-shot through the chest. . . .

"The burial party were then at work; and no doubt Colonel Shaw was buried just beyond the ditch of the fort in the trench I saw our dead indiscriminately thrown."

A Confederate officer said Shaw's body was stripped of most of his clothing, then thrown into a pit with members of the 54th as a gesture of humiliation because he commanded black troops.

"All the officers killed in the assault were decently buried, excepting Colonel Shaw," Luck wrote.

The Rebel commander reportedly said, in answer to Union requests for the return of Shaw's body, "We have buried him with his niggers!"

The words became a rallying cry for angry Northerners, and Shaw's father refused to give permission for his son's body to be reburied when Union forces occupied the fort later in the year.

"We hold that a soldier's most appropriate burial-place is on the field where he has fallen," the elder Shaw wrote General Gillmore on behalf of the family. "I shall therefore be much obliged, general, if . . . you will forbid the desecration of my son's grave, and prevent the disturbance of his remains or those buried with him."

The family's wish was granted. Shaw and the soldiers buried with him still lie beneath the sands where they fought. The ocean has encroached upon the shore, so that their graves now lie beneath 15 feet of water.

When George Stearns heard about the bloodshed,

he wrote in anguish: "I feel that they are my children whom I induced to rush into the jaws of death."

Despite the efforts of General Stevenson and the men of the 97th Pennsylvania, approximately 50 of the 54th's wounded were captured. They were taken, along with 40 of their unwounded comrades and scores of white soldiers, to the Charleston Jail.

"We were led through the lighted streets of the city, whites and blacks together, while the citizens looked on and jeered and derided," said Chaplain H. Clay Trumbull of the 10th Connecticut. "The battle of Fort Wagner was the first one in which negro soldiers were taken prisoners, and the feeling against the employing of such troops was strong and bitter in the South. The Yankees and negro soldiers now marched through the streets of Charleston represented everything that was most hateful to the Southern mind."

Charleston Jail was a five-story brick structure surrounded by a brick wall 12-feet high. Massive iron doors shut off the corridors and rooms. Here the men were confined with prostitutes, Rebel deserters, murderers, and other criminals.

And so the worst nightmare of the black soldiers had come true. In the city of slave pens and auction blocks, where they had dreamed of coming as liberators, they now faced the prospect of being sold into slavery or executed for daring to fight to free others from slavery.

Lieutenant Colonel Hallowell, who was placed in

command of the regiment after Shaw's death, singled out Sergeant Simmons, Sergeant Carney, Corporal Peal, and Private Wilson for special merit for their part in the battle.

But now Sergeant Simmons was wounded and captured. While his nephew lay dying in New York City from the mob beating he had received, Simmons lay with a wounded arm in the heat and darkness of the Charleston Jail. Later he was taken from there to a former slave market that had been converted into a prison hospital, and was now overflowing with Union wounded.

"One hundred and sixty-three of them were here," said Chaplain Trumbull, who was placed in a room so crowded with black and white soldiers there was no room to lie down.

The heat was suffocating and the wounded, who weren't taken to the hospital until two days after the battle, lay unwashed and in their blood-soaked clothing.

"In the yard of the building back of this room were six operating-tables, at which a force of busy surgeons was constantly at work," Chaplain Trumbull wrote. "Men were sinking from the shock of the operation, or from their original wounds, and closing their eyes to earth . . ."

In two days over 100 amputations were performed. Sergeant Simmons' arm, which had not bothered him much at first, grew steadily more painful and was removed. A few days later he died, not knowing what had happened to his nephew in New York City.

The doctors tended to all the white wounded before they began treating any members of the 54th. The Confederates agreed to return 105 wounded white soldiers in exchange for 38 wounded Confederates, but refused to return any of the black soldiers.

Union commanders and friends of the 54th were now more worried than ever about the fate of the men. There had already been reports that 50 captured black soldiers and two of their white officers had been hung at Milliken's Bend in Louisiana the month before.

"I feel no inclination to retaliate for offences of irresponsible persons, but, if it is the policy of any general intrusted with the command of troops, to show no quarter, or to punish with death, prisoners taken in battle, *I will accept the issue*," an angry General Ulysses S. Grant wrote the Southern commander.

"It may be you propose a different line of policy to black troops, and officers commanding them, to that practised toward white troops. If so, I can assure you that these colored troops are regularly mustered into the service of the United States. The government, and all officers under the government, are bound to give the same protection to these troops that they do to any other troops."

As soon as Governor Andrew heard that members of the 54th were in Confederate hands, he pleaded with Lincoln to take steps to protect them. Lincoln did not immediately reply, however.

Frederick Douglass told Stearns he would not recruit any more black soldiers until Lincoln promised to protect them.

"How many 54ths must be cut to pieces, its mutilated prisoners killed, and its living sold into slavery, to be tortured to death by inches, before Mr. Lincoln shall say, 'Hold, enough!' " he demanded.

Company F's Private Alexander Johnson was not captured, but his mother wrote Lincoln to express concern for his friends who'd been taken prisoner.

"I thought of this thing before I let my boy go but then they said Mr. Lincoln will never let them sell our colored soldiers for slaves," she said. "If they do he will get them back quick. He will rettallyate [retaliate] and stop it. You ought to do this, and do it at once. Not let the thing run along. Meet it quickly and manfully, and stop this, mean cowardly cruelty. We poor oppressed ones, appeal to you, and ask fair play."

General Pierre Gustave Toutant Beauregard, the Confederate commander at Charleston, wanted the captured soldiers killed immediately by strangulation.

"Let the execution be with the garrote," he declared. But Beauregard wasn't sure of official policy, and decided to ask for instructions.

"What shall be done with the negro prisoners who say they are free?" he wired Confederate Secretary of War James A. Seddon.

"They are to be handed over to the authorities of the State where captured to be dealt with according to the laws thereof," Seddon wired back.

Lincoln's Assistant Secretary of War, Charles A. Dana, told administration officials the soldiers would "probably be sold."

General Beauregard had earlier threatened to hang a captured white officer for "inciting negro slaves to insurrection." Now, however, Confederate officers were beginning to worry about Union retaliation if they sold or executed the black soldiers. They also feared that such a policy might make black soldiers fight even harder in the future, knowing they faced certain death if captured.

"A few examples might perhaps be made," a Confederate official said, "but to refuse them quarter would only make them, against their tendencies, fight desperately."

Governor M.L. Bonham of South Carolina demanded that the men be turned over to him for trial and hung if found guilty. A test case was decided on, and the first men chosen to stand trial, apparently because they were suspected of being ex-slaves, were Henry Kirk, William Harrison, and Henry Worthington of Company H, and George Counsel of Company B.

Trial was to be held in the Charleston Police Court, where black civilians who committed crimes were tried. The court's decisions were not subject to appeal.

There were two charges against the soldiers: first,

that being slaves, they were in insurrection against the state for fighting against slavery; and second, that they had been "concerned and connected" with slaves in insurrection.

A young white lawyer came to the jail and offered to defend the soldiers. At first they thought he was a government informer who wanted to find out if any of them had been slaves, but gradually he gained their confidence.

The lawyer's name was Nelson Mitchell. His property had been taken from him soon after the war began because he was considered an abolitionist and therefore a traitor to the South. Twice a secret military court sentenced him to be hung, but no one could be found to carry out the job.

Mitchell gave money to the men so they could buy extra food to supplement the small amount of cornmeal that was their only ration.

And so a lawyer who was an outcast among the people he had grown up with and in constant danger of assassination, pleaded the cause of the soldiers.

"Mitchell did all this without pay, and was very kind to us at all times," remembered Company B's Private States.

Before the trial began, officials built a gallows in the jailyard in full view of the men, and constantly taunted them about their impending deaths.

But Mitchell's eloquence on their behalf, said one man who was there, "was perfectly startling."

In addition, Confederate military leaders were

more concerned than ever over repercussions if they hung black soldiers.

Less then two weeks after the men were captured, Lincoln issued a proclamation saying that "for every soldier of the United States killed in violation of the laws of war, a Rebel soldier shall be executed, and for every one enslaved by the enemy or sold into slavery, a Rebel soldier shall be placed at hard labor until the other shall be released and receive the treatment due a prisoner of war."

Jefferson Davis was rapidly retreating from his position that the soldiers should be punished, and Secretary Seddon urged Governor Bonham not to bring them to trial "or, if condemned, that your power of executive clemency be exercised to suspend their execution, to allow the possibility of arrangement on this question, so fraught with present difficulty and future danger."

The governor also received an emotional appeal from his cousin, Sallie Butler, urging him not to hang the soldiers.

"I have been asked by a member of Campbell Williams' family to write and beg you to spare these negroes on *his* account," she said. "He is a prisoner in the hands of the Yankees, & has been selected to be *hung* in retaliation for those negroes which we have taken. . . . He is so *young* and so dear to his family."

After a trial lasting five days, the five-man tribunal of judges decided it had no jurisdiction in the case.

Mitchell's defense, said the observer, "had the effect of awaking the jury so much to the importance of the decision that I suppose they were really frightened into a favorable verdict."

Bonham said the decision "may be questioned," but announced he would not put any more of the soldiers on trial.

Though it was almost midnight when Mitchell learned of the verdict, he hurried to the jail "and called up . . . , 'All of you can now rejoice. You are recognized as United States soldiers.' "

Mitchell would soon die, penniless and despised by many of his Charleston neighbors. His death came on the same night his home was destroyed during a Union bombardment.

A few weeks before the trial, a newspaper in Virginia had written: "The very foundation of slavery would be fatally wounded if we were insane enough to treat black men as the equal of white, and insurgent slaves as equivalent to our brave white soldiers."

But now necessity forced the South to accord black men official recognition as soldiers, though many would still be murdered after capture in the battles to come. The South would also wait more than a year before transferring the men of the 54th to a prisoner of war camp, and all that time they would still threaten them with hanging.

Though the imprisoned soldiers did not know it yet, their courage at Wagner helped pave the way for widespread black participation in what was now a war of liberation, rather than a war solely to save the Union.

Northerners were deeply impressed by reports such as that given by Pierce in a letter to Governor Andrew: "Could anyone from the North see these brave fellows as they lie here, his prejudice against them if he had any, would all pass away."

Their actions, wrote an historian about the 54th, "moved the hearts and swayed the minds of the Northern people to an appreciation of the colored soldier, to a vital recognition of the end which Lincoln strove for and to the purpose of fighting out the war until the negro should be free."

Wagner marked a turning point in the war. Combined with widespread revulsion at the barbarity of the anti-black riots, it greatly strengthened support for Lincoln's policy of emancipation and the use of black soldiers to help end Southern rebellion.

"On every inch of the sands in front of Fort Wagner will be forever traced in undying glory the story of the determination and courage of these men," General Seymour cabled Washington immediately after the battle.

The pathway that they blazed would soon be followed by others, while the nation looked on in approval. Within six months, there were 60 black regiments in the army. None but the most biased now questioned the ability of black men to fight or the wisdom of using them to save the Union.

Though few Americans knew it, black men had

helped lead armies of liberation in Mexico, Venezuela, and other Latin American countries, decades before the 54th was formed. Now black men in the United States had proven *their* dedication to the cause of liberty.

"Through the cannon smoke of that black night, the manhood of the colored race shines before many eyes that would not see," declared a writer for the *Atlantic Monthly*.

In defeat, Shaw and the men of the 54th had created a legend.

9
"Are We Soldiers or Are We LABOURERS?"

I still feel more Eager for the struggle than I ever yet have, for I now wish to have Revenge for our gallant Colonel and the spilt blood of our Captain," wrote Company I's Sergeant Albanus Fisher two weeks after the battle. "We expect to Plant the Stars and Stripes on the City of Charleston."

The men of the 54th shared Fisher's feelings, even though so many of their comrades had been killed, wounded, or captured that the regiment was just a shadow of the unit that marched so triumphantly through Boston.

Each man had friends he missed, but there was little time to grieve. The Union command was now determined to crush Fort Wagner by bombarding it until only a mass of rubble remained.

The digging and fortifying of heavy siege gun emplacements called for the 54th and every other regiment to engage in backbreaking labor. They began just one day after the battle, while men were still drifting back to the unit. They began after what one officer called "the saddest [day] in the history of the Fifty-fourth, for the depleted ranks bore silent witness to the severe losses of the previous day."

General Gillmore's plan called for building three lines of guns pointing at Wagner. The first would be 1,350 yards from the fort and contain 21 guns. The second would run parallel to the first 950 yards from the fort and contain 25 guns. The third, called the "Surf Battery," would run parallel to the ocean beginning just 400 yards from Wagner and contain 25 guns.

As many men as possible were needed to build the lines and transport material, ammunition, and supplies as quickly as possible. Once the work began, it moved forward day and night.

"The weather was excessively hot, and flies and sand-fleas tormenting," said Captain Emilio. "Only sea-bathing and cooler nights made living endurable."

For almost a month no rain fell; sand particles covered everything and made the men grope blindly while they worked. There was no time for anything except long hours of work and a few hours of rest. Soon the men were in rags and their shoes were worn out.

"We have been steadily working night and day under fire," wrote one man. "And such work! Up to our knees in mud half the time, causing the wearing out of more than the volunteer's yearly allowance of clothing. . . ."

At the same time, the Confederates were busy strengthening Wagner, Sumter, and the other forts that guarded Charleston in anticipation of a new Union attack.

Eight days after the charge against Wagner, Confederate heavy guns opened fire on members of the 54th and workers from other regiments. The shovel was becoming as important as the gun, and men could die as readily while wielding one as the other.

By August 1, the strength of the 54th was up to about 600 men, and though many were still sick and weak, all tried to work.

The Confederates began using sharpshooters to try and kill members of the working details. In return, each Union company chose two men to act as sharpshooters to pick off the Rebels.

Corporal Peal was one of those chosen to act as a lookout. He was stationed on a high point where he could see the enemy batteries. Each time they fired there was a puff of smoke.

As soon as Peal saw the smoke he yelled "Cover!" and dove into a trench. At the same time, the soldiers threw their shovels aside and leaped for shelter. After the shell landed, Peal went back to his post and the men resumed their work.

Soon they began building the "Swamp Angel," a massive gun that became famous throughout the North. It was so powerful it could hurl 300-pound shells into Charleston over four miles away.

The guns had to be hauled through sinking sand, and tons of shot, shell, and powder had to be carried by hand.

"In all this work preparatory to breaching Sumter the Fifty-fourth had borne more than its share of labor," Emilio reported, "for it was exclusively employed on fatigue duty, which was not the case with the white troops."

While all this was going on, the men were again informed that they would be paid only $7 a month. By contrast, white soldiers were paid the following, plus a clothing allowance: privates and corporals, $13; sergeants, $17; first sergeants, $20; quartermaster sergeants, $21; and sergeant majors, $21. Officers, of course, received much more.

Every black soldier, from private to sergeant to chaplain to doctor (there were eventually eight in the army), received the same $7 pay each month.

Shaw had written Governor Andrew in early July that the men should either be "mustered out of the service or receive the full pay which was promised to them." Before Andrew could reply, Shaw was dead.

Sergeant Swails and many others learned that their families had been placed in the poorhouse.

"Oh, what a shame it is to be treated thus!" wrote

one soldier. "Some of us have wives and children, who are looking for succor and support from their husbands and fathers; but, alas! they look in vain."

Mary Livermore, a volunteer with the Sanitary Commission in Chicago — a forerunner to the American Red Cross — told of a visit to one of the wives.

"Since her husband's absence, she has passed through hunger, cold, sickness, and bereavement," Livermore said of the woman, whom she didn't identify. "Her landlord, a rich man of the city . . . put her out of her house on the sidewalk, in a cold rain storm, because she owed him five dollars for rent, and could not then earn it, as her child was sick unto death with scarlet fever.

"One of her colored neighbors, as poor as she, took her in; and the baby died on the next Sunday morning. She came to me to get the baby buried, without going to the poormaster. 'It don't seem right for my child to be buried like a pauper,' she said, 'when her father is fighting for the country.' And I agreed with her."

Governor Andrew was furious when he heard of the suffering of the families and gave Livermore "carte blanche for the relief of the families living in Chicago whose husbands and fathers have enlisted in the Fifty-fourth."

He also fired off an angry letter to President Lincoln declaring that the soldiers "stand in every respect . . . upon the same laws which support the rights of white soldiers . . . the laws for the payment of the volunteer army of the United States apply to these men, or they apply to nobody."

The government still refused to give them the same pay as whites, however, and the Massachusetts legislature voted to provide the difference.

The men turned down this arrangement, saying they were not willing "that the Federal Government should throw mud upon them, even though Massachusetts stands ready to wipe it off. . . . The regiment whose bayonets pricked the name of Colonel Shaw into the roll of immortal honor can afford to be cheated out of their money, but not out of their manhood."

The 54th was now part of a new all-black brigade that also included the 2nd South Carolina and the 3rd United States Colored Troops, under the command of Colonel Montgomery.

Montgomery lashed out at the men for their stand.

"You must remember you have not proved yourselves as soldiers," he told them. "Nor should you expect to be placed on the same footing with white men. Any one listening to your shouting and singing can see how grotesquely ignorant you are. . . . In refusing to take the pay offered you, and what you are only legally entitled to, you are guilty of insubordination and can be tried and shot by court-martial."

An officer who was present said Montgomery also made insulting comments about the light skin color of many of the men. But still they stood firm and one of them appealed directly to President Lincoln for justice.

"The main question is, Are we *Soldiers* or are we LABOURERS," wrote Corporal James Gooding of Company C, the New Bedford company. "We have done a Soldiers Duty. Why can't we have a Soldiers pay?"

In spite of all these appeals, black soldiers continued to be denied equal pay.

Members of the 3rd South Carolina Regiment, comprised entirely of ex-slaves, laid down their arms and said they wouldn't fight until they were given equal pay. Sergeant William Walker was charged with being the ringleader and executed for mutiny.

When Governor Andrew heard of Walker's death, he said sarcastically, "The Government which found no law to pay him except as a nondescript and a contraband [ex-slave], nevertheless found law enough to shoot him as a soldier."

The 55th Massachusetts Colored Regiment soon arrived, and soldiers from both outfits sent an impassioned letter to Congress.

But the majority of congressmen remained unmoved, and the men concentrated on the work of building the Swamp Angel and the other batteries. Increasingly, because of the heavy shelling from Forts Sumter, Wagner, and Gregg, the men worked mainly at night when they could see the lighted shells and tell where they were headed.

On August 17 the first bombardment of Fort Sumter began, and by nightfall, said one of the officers, the walls "looked like a honeycomb."

A giant siege gun was brought up. It was moved only at night and covered with grass to hide it in the daytime. By the time it was ready to fire, the men had expended the equivalent of 2,500 days of labor on it.

At last all the guns were ready. General Gillmore ordered a powerful calcium light to shine on Wagner so it could be bombarded by night as well as day. At the same time he ordered the 54th divided into four equal parts, with each of the groups to spend eight hours in the forward trenches.

It was desirable, wrote Major T.B. Brooks, the assistant engineer, "to have older troops for the important and hazardous duty required at this period."

The engineers would blow open the ground with explosives. Then the 54th and other troops would follow to widen the trenches and build sand barriers to provide cover from Rebel sharpshooters.

On September 1, the bombardment of Wagner began. The fire came from land and sea, and it was more intense than anything the fort's defenders had ever seen before.

Starting with early dawn, said one Confederate soldier, the shelling shook the fort "to its centre . . . . The burning sun of a Southern summer, its heat intensified by the reflection of the white sand, scorched and blistered the unprotected garrison. . . .

"Water was scarcer than whiskey. . . . The un-ventilated bombproofs, filled with smoke of lamps and smell of blood, were intolerable, so that one endured the risk of shot and shell rather than seek their shelter."

For six days the fierce bombardment continued, and piece by piece the fort was thrown down as if by a giant hand.

The last day of the siege was September 6. General Gillmore issued an order for Wagner to be assaulted at nine o'clock the next morning, the hour of low tide. He had learned something from the first assault, when many of the attackers met death as they struggled through high tide.

At two o'clock the men of the 54th were awakened and formed into battle lines in the darkness. Captain Joseph Walker of the 1st New York Engineers and a captain from the 55th Massachusetts, crawled out to the ditch where so many men had died that awful night. There they pulled up 200 spears and stakes.

Engineers set off explosions to level the earth, so that the attackers could run over it quickly.

But no sound or shots came from Wagner. For 20 minutes, in preparation for the assault, every Union gun fired on Wagner. Then volunteers were asked to go into the fort and report on what they found.

Five men responded. In a few minutes they came back and said Wagner was deserted. Unknown to the Union forces, the Confederate commander told his superiors his troops could not stand another day of bombardment. In a single day, 100 of his 900 troops had been wounded or killed. In addition, he said, the Rebels' black laborers absolutely refused to work any longer.

So when nightfall came, the Confederates quietly abandoned the fort that had taken so many Union lives less than two months before.

It was dawn when the volunteers reported back, and when the waiting troops heard the news, they danced and shouted for joy.

Wagner had fallen at last.

It had taken 58 days from the time of the 54th's assault on the evening of July 18. It had taken 19,000 days of work performed by the infantry. Half that work was done by black troops, even though there were ten times as many whites.

Nathaniel Paige of the *New York Tribune* reported that the black soldiers "were under fire at Morris Island for two months while performing sixteen hours labor per day; during this period the white troops were unable to accomplish over eight to ten hours' labor per diem."

General Gillmore finally issued the following order: "Colored troops will not be required to perform any labor which is not shared by the white troops, but will receive in all respects the same treatment, and be allowed the same opportunities for drill and instruction."

In his official report on the operation, Major Brooks said: "It is probable that in no military operations of the war have negro troops done so large a proportion, and so important and hazardous fatigue duty, as in the siege operations on the island."

Their work had paid off. Now soldiers from the 54th guarded Fort Wagner, making their rounds in sunshine and moonlight above the sands where their friends lay buried.

"Fort Sumter is destroyed," General Gillmore proclaimed in an order to his troops. "The scene where our country's flag suffered its first dishonor you have made the theatre of one of its proudest triumphs . . . and [rescued] the graves of your fallen comrades. . . .

"The city and harbor of Charleston lie at the mercy of your artillery from the very spot where the first shot was fired at your country's flag and the Rebellion itself was inaugurated."

General Gillmore ordered that his personal gifts of "medals of honor" [Gillmore Medals] be presented to Corporal Peal, Sergeant Carney, Sergeant Simmons, and Private Wilson, so they could be "recorded above their fellows for special merit." The captured Simmons died without knowing he had been honored.

It had been a long and deadly summer, but at last it was over. Many eager young men were dead and many new recruits had come to take their places. Soon they, too, would hear the sound of battle and know its pain.

Soon they, too, would willingly risk their lives in the struggle to free a nation.

10
"History Records
a Noble Deed"

Autumn came, and with it increased Union artillery attacks on Charleston. The land-based siege guns and navy warships bombarded the city day and night, often setting fires that blazed along the wharves or among the houses.

There was no special celebration on Christmas Day, but New Year's 1864, was different. It was the first anniversary of the Emancipation Proclamation.

The men of the 54th gathered on the parade ground to listen to speeches celebrating issuance of the proclamation. Sergeant Joseph Barquet of Company H, a 40-year-old mason from Galesburg, Illinois, was the featured speaker.

Barquet stood on the upturned wooden box that served as the speakers' platform and launched into a passionate oration. In the middle of it, the box collapsed and Barquet disappeared.

"Gentlemen," he called out from inside the box. "I admire your principles, but damn your platform!"

For several weeks work crews had been busy repairing Wagner and positioning guns within its walls. Finally, on January 12, the Stars and Stripes was officially raised on a newly erected flagpole. A few days later the 54th was brought back up to full strength with the arrival from Boston of 112 recruits.

A week later the regiment received orders to embark for Florida as soon as ships were available. Two steamers, the *J.B. Collins* and the *Monohansett*, arrived on the 28th and departed the next day at high tide.

President Lincoln wanted to make Florida into a state loyal to the Union, plus seize its raw materials. So with Lincoln's permission General Gillmore assembled a force of 7,000 men backed by 28 transports and navy warships. General Seymour, who commanded the assault on Wagner in July, was placed in charge.

The expedition landed at Jacksonville, and Colonel Hallowell was named commandant of the town. This was the fourth time Union forces had occupied Jacksonville, and much of it lay in ruins.

On February 20 at about 1:30 P.M., the Union and Confederate armies met near a railroad 50 miles west of the city.

The North would call the fight the Battle of Olustee, while the South named it the Battle of Ocean Pond because of a large lake near one end of the battlefield.

The 54th was ordered to wait as a reserve force in the rear, and the men rested in the shade as the battle began in the distance. At first they heard only the small arms fire, but soon the cannons began to boom.

"That's home-made thunder," one man joked.

"I don't mind the thunder if the lightning don't strike me!" his friend replied.

Things began to go wrong almost immediately. The men of the 7th New Hampshire, apparently mistaking an order to move forward, instead scattered to the rear and could not be stopped.

The 7th Connecticut and 8th U.S. Colored tried to hold their ground despite heavy losses, but were finally forced to retreat.

It was almost 2:30 P.M.

A messenger on horseback raced to where the 54th was resting, with orders from Seymour to move into battle at double-quick time. Within moments the men were running forward, forcing their way through hundreds of wounded soldiers and men who refused to fight anymore.

"You'll all get killed," some of them yelled at the 54th.

The men reached the field hospital of the 8th U.S. Colored just as it was about to be captured by the Confederates. They raced past it, closing with the Rebel troops as 18-year-old Sergeant Garnet Cezar of Company D led them in shouting their new battle cry: "Three cheers for Massachusetts and seven dollars a month!"

Corporal Peal carried the state flag and Sergeant James Wilkins, a 21-year-old from Company D, carried the Stars and Stripes.

Seymour rode up to Hallowell and told him the army would be annihilated unless the 54th could hold the Rebels long enough for a new battle line to be formed in the rear.

There were now 497 enlisted men and 13 officers in the 54th formed for battle in an open pine forest. Confederate sharpshooters in the trees hit several men, but were soon brought down by accurate volleys.

The 1st North Carolina Colored came up and fought valiantly beside the 54th, but suffered devastating losses and was forced to retire. The 1st North Carolina's casualties totaled 242 officers and enlisted men killed or wounded, including a fatal wound to its commanding officer.

While the battle raged, the 54th band "took position on the side of the road" and soon "The Star-Spangled Banner" burst out "on the sulphureous air, amid the roar of artillery, the rattle of musketry and the shouts of commands, mingling its soul-stirring strains with the deafening yells of the charging columns. . . . Its thrilling notes, soaring above the battle's gales, aroused to new life and renewed energy the panting, routed troops. . . ."

With the departure of the 1st North Carolina, the

54th was left alone to hold back the Confederates.
So exposed were the soldiers' positions that one of
the officers speculated the regiment was either forgotten or considered a necessary sacrifice to give the
rest of the army time to retreat.

As the men stood alone facing the enemy in the
deepening twilight, they were ordered to give nine
loud cheers to make the Confederates think reinforcements had arrived. Then under cover of darkness the regiment hurriedly marched to the rear,
stopping every two or three hundred yards to face
forward ready to do battle. They were not pursued,
however.

"The two colored regiments had stood in the gap
and saved the army," a newspaper correspondent
reported.

The scene in the rear was one of chaos, with men
and horsedrawn wagons and carts clogging the narrow road. The wounded and the weary who were
unable to proceed any further sprawled on both sides
of the road.

Men stampeded through the night, throwing away
anything that would slow them down. Lieutenant
Appleton, using the 54th as a nucleus, gathered
those who were able-bodied and formed a rearguard
to help protect the retreating army.

At 2 A.M. the 54th reached Barber's, after marching 32 miles in 24 hours. It had been, said one man,
"a fight, a licking and a foot race."

At 9 A.M. the men of the 54th moved out, and

began a march of 22 miles. Seymour ordered them to turn around, however, and retrace their steps. Over 300 wounded lay on railroad flatcars, but the locomotive had broken down and the helpless soldiers were in danger of being captured.

"Through eagerness to escape the supposed pursuing enemy, too great pressure of steam was employed, and the flue collapsed," said one man. "And here the immortal Fifty-fourth (colored) did what ought to insure it higher praise than to hold the field in the face of a victorious foe — with ropes it seized the engine (now useless) and dragged it with its doomed freight for many miles. . . . They knew their fate if captured; their humanity triumphed. Does history record a nobler deed?"

One of their officers said the men "faced about cheerfully" when ordered to march back to the train, even though they were exhausted and hadn't eaten since before the battle.

They searched out and loaded more wounded, and some even cut vines to use to help pull the train. Finally, on the evening of the 22nd, the 54th reached Jacksonville.

"The 54th marched 120 miles in 102 hours, yet the roll-call showed no stragglers," the Adjutant General of Massachusetts said in his official report.

The regiment's casualty list was 13 killed, 63 wounded, and 8 missing. One of the missing was Corporal Gooding.

Two hundred and fifty of the Union wounded were

immediately taken by ship to Beaufort, where Colonel Higginson visited them as soon as they arrived.

The conduct of Sergeant Swails led the officers of the 54th to recommend his promotion as the regiment's first black officer. When enlisted men were promoted to officers, they first had to be discharged from their present rank and then mustered into their regiment with an officer's rank.

Colonel Hallowell forwarded the recommendation to Governor Andrew, who endorsed it. But General John Foster, who had warned Jefferson Davis to treat black soldiers on an equal basis with whites, refused to discharge Swails because he had "partial African blood." Secretary Stanton approved of Foster's action.

"How can we hope for success to our arms or Gods blessing in any shape while we as a nation are so blind to justice?" Hallowell wrote Andrew in protest.

Even though much of the prejudice against black soldiers had lessened, much still remained.

Lincoln said he had even been advised by some opponents of racial equality to "return to slavery the black warriors of . . . Olustee. I should be damned in time & in eternity for so doing. The world shall know that I will keep my faith to friends & enemies, come what will."

Congress continued to refuse to give black soldiers equal pay and the men were getting increasingly restless over the unsettled pay issue, leading one officer to fear they would mutiny. Colonel Hallowell said that two men, who had shown a "disposition" to mutiny, had been shot and slightly wounded.

"Letters have been constantly arriving for six months in these regiments [the 54th and 55th], in which the wives of the enlisted men describe their sufferings, and the sufferings of their families," wrote the general commanding the regiments. "Children have died because they could not be supplied with proper food, and because the Doctor could not be paid, or medicines obtained from the Druggist . . . wives have proved untrue to their husbands and abandoned their offspring. Mothers advise their sons to throw down the musket and come home, it being impossible for them to live longer without their support."

Secretary Stanton urged Congress to correct the inequity. Congress finally passed a law in June 1864 granting equal pay to black soldiers who had been free on April 19, 1861, the week after the war began.

Most soldiers in other black regiments were still slaves then, and even some in the 54th were not free on that date. The law would still call for these men to be paid as laborers.

Colonel Hallowell, a Quaker, made up what became widely known as "the Quaker's Oath," as a way to get around this provison in the law:

"You do solemnly swear that you owed no man unrequited labor on or before the 19th day of April, 1861. So help you God."

Governor Andrew approved of the oath and all the men swore to it with a clear conscience.

"That they were compelled to take this or any oath at the last was an insult crowning the injury," said an officer.

Colonel Higginson, whose regiment was composed almost entirely of ex-slaves, was livid at the distinction Congress made between black soldiers who had been free and those who had been enslaved when the war began.

The men in his command enlisted because they trusted the government's honor, he said. "Now the nation turns upon them and says: Your part of the contract is fulfilled; we have had your services. If you can show that you had previously been free for a certain length of time, we will fulfill the other side of the contract. If not, we repudiate it. Help yourselves if you can."

The political reality of anti-black racism, even though it had lessened because of the deeds of black soldiers, continued to dictate how they were treated by the government.

Governor Andrew stated the issue clearly when he said: "For fear the uniform may dignify the enfranchised slave, or make the black man seem like a free citizen, the government means to disgrace and degrade him, so that he may always be in his own eyes, and in the eyes of all men, 'only a nigger.' "

At last, though, there was at least some progress.

On September 28, 1864, the regiment assembled for their first pay since enlisting. That day and the next day they received a total of $170,000 and sent their loved ones $100,000 of it.

"We had been eighteen months waiting, and the kaleidoscope was turned—nine hundred men received their money; nine hundred stories rested on the faces of those men, as they passed in at one door and out of the other," wrote one of the officers. "There was use in waiting! Two days have changed the face of things, and now a petty carnival prevails.

"The fiddle and other music long neglected enlivens the tents day and night. Songs burst out everywhere; dancing is incessant; boisterous shouts are heard, mimicry, burlesque, and carnival; pompous salutations are heard on all sides. Here a crowd and a preacher; there a crowd and two boxers; yonder, feasting and jubilee."

And at last Sergeant Swails was permitted to become Second Lieutenant Swails, thanks in part to the fact that he was light-skinned.

"Sergt. Swails is so nearly white that it would be difficult to discover any trace of his African blood," wrote General Foster. "He is so intelligent and of such good character that after a fair trial I now recommend his being allowed to serve as a commissioned officer."

Swails was not commissioned until the war was almost over, which was the case with most of the fewer than 100 black men given Union officer's commissions in the Civil War. (There were over 7,000 white officers in the black regiments.)

Commissioning a black man could result in his

sometimes having authority over whites, and this was something the United States was not willing to let happen until the Korean War in 1950.

As the war neared its end, there had been progress for black soldiers both in commissions and pay, but for many it was too late.

Each soldier who died before the pay issue was settled died, said Higginson, "defrauded by the Government of nearly one half his petty pay."

Corporal Peal lingered for several weeks, then died from the wounds he received at Olustee. Word was eventually received that Corporal Gooding had died at the infamous Confederate prisoner-of-war camp at Andersonville, Georgia: one of over 12,000 Union soldiers who died there.

Peal from Oberlin and Gooding from New Bedford had both fought bravely at Wagner and Olustee, earning the praise of their comrades and officers. But both died without having ever received a cent from the government that accepted their services and their lives.

They had indeed earned the right, as General Gillmore said, to be "recorded above their fellows for special merit." Peal was buried with a soldier's honors in the military cemetery at Beaufort. Gooding's body was never found.

Their lives and their deaths had helped bring nearer the moment they both dreamed of, when the walls of slavery would be cast down and the slaves set free.

11
"Keeping Step
to Freedom's Drumbeat"

Charleston was being steadily pounded into submission by the guns of the Union army and navy. Fires sprang up constantly and supplies were running low.

In a desperate attempt to stop the bombardment, the Confederates built a stockade near the waterfront and filled it with captured Union officers.

The Union Army quickly retaliated by building a stockade enclosed by 10-foot-high pine posts, just north of Fort Wagner. It was 228 feet by 304 feet, and directly exposed to Confederate fire. A platform for guards ran atop the posts, and a "dead line" was marked off by rope 20 feet inside the posts. Anyone who crossed the line would be shot. A battery of artillery faced the only gate.

The 54th was assigned to guard the 560 Confederate officers chosen as prisoners.

On September 7, the prisoners arrived on the steamer *Cossack*, and were marched to the open-air prison by black soldiers. Two companies of the 54th guarded them on either side. Three companies of the 21st U.S. Colored Troops led the way, while two companies of the 21st guarded the rear. It was a procession soldiers from both the Union and Confederacy would have thought impossible when the war began.

The prisoners lived in tents and had to answer a roll call three times a day. They were fed one-half the regular army ration at first, then less than that to match the rations given captured Union officers. Breakfast and dinner consisted of one cracker apiece, while lunch was two crackers with a little meat and beans.

At night the stockade was brightly illuminated by a calcium light placed atop Fort Wagner's parapet.

The men of the 54th guarded the prisoners "near the grave of their beloved Colonel Shaw," Hallowell wrote Governor Andrew. "Some of these same rebel officers were in Fort Wagner on the memorable night when we assaulted it and say they saw Colonel Shaw fall. . . .

"Our men are proud of the honor of guarding these Rebels but they do not like to *see* them starved even in retaliation. When off duty they say it is all right, but when on duty if a man begs them for something to eat, it is hard not to be allowed to yield to the feeling which prompts them to do good to those who despitefully use them."

After several weeks, General Foster was informed that the Confederate commander had taken the captured Union officers out of the line of fire. Foster then ordered the Confederates removed from the stockade and placed in a regular prisoner-of-war camp.

During all the time the 54th guarded the captured officers, there were no escapes, no disturbances, and no complaints of harsh treatment.

"The brigadier-general commanding desires me . . . to tender you his sincere thanks for the prompt and efficient manner in which you and the officers and men of your command discharged their duties while guarding the Rebel prisoners-of-war," a member of the adjutant general's staff wrote Hallowell.

In the fall of 1864, President Lincoln was reelected along with anti-slavery politicians in several states, ending the South's last hope to save their Confederacy by political compromise. The men of the 54th and their officers now felt confident the war would be brought to a swift conclusion.

All across the South the Confederacy was crumbling.

Atlanta had fallen to Union forces, who raised

the American flag over city hall. The Army of the Potomac, accompanied by General Grant, was threatening Petersburg and the Confederate capital at Richmond.

The forces of General William T. Sherman were burning a 60-mile-wide path of destruction across the South on their famous "march to the sea." They were expected to head for Charleston and its 10,000 Confederate troops.

Instead of turning toward Charleston, however, Sherman attacked toward the center of the state: He wanted to destroy the railroad connecting Charleston and the state capital at Columbia.

"If I am able to reach certain vital points," Sherman said, "Charleston will fall of itself."

He sent a telegram to the Union command saying: "I would like to have Foster break the Charleston and Savannah Railroad about Pocotaligo about the 1st of December."

As a result, eight companies of the 54th joined over 4,000 other Union troops in sailing from Hilton Head several miles inland on the Broad River. Companies B and F stayed behind.

The army went ashore at a dilapidated wharf called Boyd's Landing, and began marching down a narrow wagon road toward the Charleston and Savannah Railroad approximately ten miles away. The 54th led the way, followed by the 55th Massachusetts, 32nd, 34th, 35th, and 102nd U.S. Colored Troops, and six white regiments.

Parts of the army became lost on crossroads, delaying the attack by several hours. Unknown to the Union command, this delay gave the Confederates much-needed time for reinforcements to arrive.

At a slight elevation called Honey Hill, the two sides met. The hill was protected by a swamp in front, while thick trees and bushes covered the defenders on top of the hill.

There was so little opposition on the approach to Honey Hill that the cheerful black soldiers "made the woods ring" with the following song, according to one of them:

> "Ho, boys, chains are breaking;
> Bondsmen fast awaking;
> Tyrant hearts are quaking;
> Southward we are making. . . .
>
> "No more for trader's gold
> Shall those we love be sold;
> Nor crushed be manhood bold
> In slavery's dreaded fold.
>   Huzza! Huzza!
>   Our song shall be
>   Huzza! Huzza!
>   THAT WE ARE FREE!"

At the foot of the hill, the black regiments were ordered to charge through the swamp and up a narrow roadway. They began the charge, but those in

the swamp soon found it impassable and could go no
further.

Suddenly "a galling fire of grape, canister, and
musketry" swept through their ranks and forced them
back.

Most of the 54th was assigned to guard commu-
nications in the rear and was not brought up until
the other regiments were forced to retreat. Their
sister regiment, the 55th, lost over 100 men in five
minutes.

Captain Pope of the 54th's Company I led his men
forward through the wagons, ambulances, and loads
of ammunition that blocked the road. When he
reached the foot of the hill he saw what a terrible
price the 55th had paid.

"How the shot tore down that hill and up the
road!" he said. "I could see where the Fifty-fifth had
charged, and their dead lying there."

Sergeant Charles W. Lenox of Company A said
the woods "were so thick in front that the movements of most of the force could not be seen. . . .
Wagner always seemed to me the most terrible of
our battles, but the musketry at Honey Hill was
something fearful. The so-called 'Rebel yell' was
more prominent than I ever heard it."

The battle began a little after 8:30 A.M. and ended
almost 12 hours later when the Union forces with-
drew under cover of darkness.

Men from the 54th searched the battlefield long
after the last ambulances had left for the rear. They

found 150 wounded and carried them several miles to a church that had been cleared of seats and converted into a hospital.

Then they chose those wounded still able to travel and carried them still further to the rear. Many of the men in the regiment made more than one trip. The attack had been a failure and the 54th lost two men killed, 38 wounded, and one captured: Private Hill Harris of Company G.

Private Harris was taken to the Charleston Jail where he joined those of his comrades captured on James Island and at Wagner. The Confederates still threatened to hang them, and they still lived in the shadow of the gallows. Finally Harris and ten others were transferred to Andersonville Prison in Andersonville, where three are known to have died. Four others were never heard from again, but Private Harris was eventually released.

Confederate forces were now on the defensive throughout the South, and though the attempt to cut the railroad had failed, the 54th soon became the first body of eastern troops to link up with Sherman's western army.

It happened on January 15, 1865, as the 54th and other regiments under General Foster's command continued to harass the Charleston and Savannah Railroad.

The previous evening pickets from the 54th, who thought they still faced the Confederate army, "were first mystified and then elated by hearing drums and

fifes far to our right and front, sounding reveille and
playing national airs."

The next morning Colonel Hallowell led the regiment forward and they soon joined with Sherman's
17th Corps.

A few days later, Captain Appleton and other
officers were playing cards at headquarters when a
middle-aged officer entered and asked for the commanding general.

"Without ceasing their card-playing, the young
officers informed the stranger of the general's absence," said Captain Emilio. "Imagine their con-
sternation when their visitor quietly said, 'Please say
to him that General Sherman called.' They started
up, ashamed and apologizing, but the general swiftly
departed as he came."

Lieutenant Colonel Henry Hooper, assistant commander of the 54th, said that everywhere Sherman's
armies went, destruction followed.

"All through the country, as far as can be seen,
pillars of black smoke rise. . . . The saying is that
'when Sherman gets through South Carolina, a crow
can't fly across the country unless he carries rations
with him.' "

The remainder of the war could now be counted
in weeks. On February 17, Sherman entered Columbia, making it impossible for the Confederates to
continue holding Charleston.

The Confederate commander ordered his troops
to evacuate the city, and burn it as they left. This

they did before daylight on the 18th, setting such huge fires that the city would have burned down if the black residents and Union soldiers hadn't put out the fires.

The 200 men of Companies B and F saw the fires burning in the night from their positions on Morris Island, and heard huge explosions as the Confederates blew up ammunition dumps and three gunboats in the harbor.

At 7:45 A.M. on the 18th, a heavy fog finally lifted. The soldiers looked through powerful binoculars, but could see no Rebel flags flying in the city or on the forts in the harbor.

They quickly raised the Stars and Stripes over the forts that had defied them so long and claimed so many of their friends. Less than three hours later they reached Charleston by rowboat. There the mayor formally surrendered, and the soldiers hoisted the American flag over city hall.

Then, clear voices ringing in the morning air and heads held high, the men marched through the streets of Charleston singing "The Battle Cry of Freedom":

> "Yes, we'll rally round the flag, boys,
>   we'll rally once again,
> Shouting the battle cry of Freedom,
> We will rally from the hillside, we'll
>   gather from the plain,
> Shouting the battle cry of Freedom.

"The Union forever, Hurrah boys, Hurrah!
Down with the traitor, Up with the star;
While we rally round the flag, boys, rally
    once again.
Shouting the battle cry of Freedom!"

Thus did black soldiers come as liberators to the
Confederacy's "Holy of Holies," the place where the
laws of secession were passed and the struggle to
maintain slavery began almost four years before.

Men of the 54th and 21st U.S. Colored Troops
entered the city as conquering heroes while the fires
raged around them and awestruck black residents
sought to touch them.

They came "offering no insult, uttering no epi-
thet, manifesting no revenge, for all the wrongs of
centuries heaped upon them by a people now hum-
bled and at their mercy," said war correspondent
Charles Coffin.

"Around them gathered a dusky crowd of men,
women and children, dancing, shouting, mad with
very joy. Mothers held up their little ones to see the
men in blue, to catch a sight of the starry flag, with
its crimson folds and tassels of gold."

Wherever the flag passed, said one man, "it was
honored with shouts and the waving of handkerchiefs and caps."

White Union soldiers who had escaped from their
captors weeks or months before, came out of hiding
and told how black residents had kept them alive.

The Company B comrades of Sergeant Simmons

joined Sergeant Henry Patterson of Oberlin and the other members of Company F as they rushed to Charleston Jail to search for their friends.

The captured soldiers had all been transferred to prisoner-of-war camps, though, but the determined soldiers hurried to the SLAVE MART on Chalmers Street. There many Charleston slavetraders had their offices in a building that also contained locked and barred slave pens.

The soldiers smashed down the doors and broke open the pens, leaving the gates in splinters on the floor. Then they left to fight the fires.

"That the whole city was not obliterated in consequence of these acts of General Beauregard and his subordinates, can only be attributed to the exertions of our soldiery and negro inhabitants," declared one officer.

Coffin said the black soldiers had already proved their valor on the battlefield, "and on this ever memorable day they made manifest to the world their superiority in honor and humanity."

They marched into the city, wrote Coffin, "keeping step to freedom's drumbeat, up the grass-grown streets, past the slave shambles, laying aside their arms, working with the fire engines to extinguish the flames, and, in the spirit of the Redeemer of men, saving that which was lost."

Many members of the 21st were born in South Carolina and had been sold from Charleston auction blocks.

One group of soldiers manning a fire pump looked

up to see an auction block on which they had stood
as slaves. They lifted it to their shoulders and carried
it to the waterfront, where it was shipped to Boston.
There it was covered with a Confederate flag captured by the 54th, and William Lloyd Garrison stood
on it to make an abolitionist speech.

Wendell Phillips, hearing of all this, asked: "Can
you conceive of a bitterer drop that God's chemistry
could mix for a son of the Palmetto State than that
a Massachusetts flag and a colored regiment should
take possession of Charleston?"

Black soldiers were appointed to keep law and
order, and guarded all the public buildings.

Coffin wrote that "whoever desired protection papers or passes, whoever had business with the marshal
or the general commanding the city, rich or poor,
high-born or low-born, white or black, man or
woman, must first meet a colored sentinel face to
face, and obtain from the colored sergeant permission to enter the gate."

The members of the 54th contributed almost
$3,000 to help open the first public school in the
city. It was attended by 1,200 black and white young-
sters, and was named the Shaw School in honor of
their beloved colonel.

The eight companies of the 54th serving with
General Foster were soon ordered to Charleston.
They had also been busy freeing slaves, helping several thousand flee the destruction of the South Carolina interior.

The final weeks of the war passed swiftly, and on April 3 Richmond fell. Three Union regiments, including the black 5th Massachusetts Cavalry led by the grandson of President John Quincy Adams, marched triumphantly into the capital of the Confederacy.

When Secretary Stanton heard the news, he ordered an 800-gun salute in the nation's capital.

Like the black residents of Charleston, those of Richmond were beside themselves with joy. They ran beside the cavalrymen cheering wildly, and the cavalrymen rose up in their stirrups and waved their swords in reply.

That same day, Major Martin Delaney entered Charleston and began enlisting ex-slaves into the Union Army. In one day, 300 men signed up. On April 14, at President Lincoln's request, a flag-raising ceremony was held at Fort Sumter.

At noon the shell-marked flag that had been lowered in surrender, was raised in triumph, to the acclamation of thousands and the roar of cannons.

Henry Ward Beecher and Garrison came from Boston for the ceremony, and Robert Smalls ferried hundreds of people from Charleston to Fort Sumter on the *Planter*, which was now a U.S. Navy vessel that he commanded as a captain.

Among Smalls' passengers were the son of Denmark Vesey, a carpenter who was hung after leading an unsuccessful slave rebellion in Charleston 43 years before, and Private Toussaint Delaney of Company

D. Though the 54th was stationed on the edge of town, Private Delaney was specially assigned to accompany his father.

Two months before, Private Delaney's father had been commissioned the first high-ranking black line officer in the army.

"You are the first of your race who has been thus honored by the government," Secretary Stanton told him. "Therefore much depends and will be expected of you."

Everywhere he went in Charleston, black people tried to touch him. They even came to his room at all hours of the day and night to see a black man wearing the shoulder tabs of a United States major. When he spoke in the city's largest black church — Zion Church — 6,000 people packed the pews, aisles, and dooryards to hear him.

Children who had been slaves a month before now crowded the streets to watch him pass. Suddenly the celebration of freedom ended when word was received that President Lincoln had been shot by Confederate sympathizer John Wilkes Booth. The next day, which was the day after the flag was raised over Fort Sumter, Lincoln died. He was succeeded as president by ex-Tennessee governor and slaveowner, Andrew Johnson.

Blacks and abolitionists throughout the nation were stunned and wondered what it all meant for the cause of freedom. Only five days before, Confederate General Robert E. Lee had been forced to surrender his Army of Northern Virginia to Grant at Appomattox Courthouse in Virginia. The war was effectively over.

Lee had ordered his army to make one last desperate attempt to break out of the Union trap almost surrounding them and try to reach the nearby mountains "at all hazards." They tried, and for awhile it seemed they would succeed.

On Palm Sunday morning, the Confederates drove back and scattered Union cavalrymen, only to find a sea of Union infantry forming battle lines to meet them 800 yards away. Black soldiers stood with white soldiers, bayonets glistening in the morning sun, blocking the way and spelling the Confederacy's doom.

"He was out-marched, out-fought, out-witted, out-generaled — defeated in every possible way," said Sergeant Major Wilson of Company B in a book he later wrote. "He and his army, every man, numbering 27,516, surrendered. He and his army, every man, was fed by the conqueror."

The war was over, though word would come too late to stop a last charge by the 54th, which had suddenly been ordered to attack a place called Boykin's Mills. Ironically for a regiment born despite reluctance to let black men fight, the battle came after everyone else had stopped fighting.

Again the regiment had to charge against an entrenched foe, this time across a narrow bridge surrounded by swampland.

"No better position could be found for a defense, as the only approach to it, was by a narrow embankment about 200 yards long, where only one could walk at a time . . . under a galling fire which swept the bridge and enbankment, rendering it a fearful 'way of death,' " wrote Sergeant Wilson.

"The heroes of Wagner and Olustee did not shrink from the trial, but actually charged in single file. The first to step upon the fatal path, went down like grass before the scythe, but over their prostrate bodies came their comrades, until the enemy, panic-stricken by such determined daring, abandoned their position and fled."

Private James Johnson of Company F, a 21-year-old barber from Owego, New York, was one of those killed. Another who fell at the mill was first Lieutenant Edward Stevens, possibly the last Union Officer killed in the war.

The next day a Confederate officer brought word under a flag of truce that the war was over. The men and officers then gathered in an open field under a rainy sky, and there "the last shots loaded with hostile intent were fired as a salute."

On the night of August 21 and the early morning of August 23, the 54th sailed for Boston on two steamers: the C.F. *Thomas* and the *Ashland*. Shortly before they left, Sergeants Vogelsang and Welch received their officers' commissions.

On September 1, final payments were made to the officers and men, and on September 2 the 54th landed at Commercial Wharf in Boston. Friends had asked that the regiment be greeted on the line of march with large crowds, refreshments, and displays of the Stars and Stripes.

They were.

The *Boston Evening Transcript* described the welcome they received as they retraced their steps of two-and-one-half years before.

> "The Fifty-fourth Massachusetts Regiment, the pioneer State colored regiment of this country, recruited at a time when great prejudices existed against enlisting any but so-called white men in the army, when a colored soldiery was considered in the light of an experiment almost certain to fail, this command — which now returns crowned with laurels, and after two hundred thousand of their brethren, from one end of the traitorous South to the other, have fought themselves into public esteem — had such a reception today as befitted an organization the history of which is admitted to form so conspicious a part of the annals of the country."

The men marched to the State House where Governor Andrew reviewed them, and where the battle-scarred flag carried by Sergeant Carney at Fort Wagner is still enshrined.

Then at last, after executing some final maneuvers while the crowd cheered, the men and officers of the regiment said their farewells and began their journeys toward the scores of cities, towns, and villages they called home.

The men of the 54th had marched, sung, and fought their way into the hearts of black and white Americans. Now the "Glory" Regiment belonged to history.

Epilogue:
"The Battle Cry
of Freedom"

The valor of the men of the 54th swept aside opposition to the use of black men as soldiers. By the end of the war, over 186,000 had served in the army (and another 30,000 in the navy), in 11 light artillery batteries and at least 140 regiments: 7 cavalry, 12 heavy artillery, and 121 infantry. (One writer listed 140 infantry regiments, but many were short-lived.)

More than 38,000 of the men died on the battlefield and from disease.

Sixteen of the soldiers won the Congressional Medal of Honor (along with seven black sailors), including Company C's Sergeant Carney, although he didn't receive it until 1897.

During the deadly fighting around Petersburg, Virginia, which helped bring the war to an end, 12 black men won the medal in one fierce day of valor: September 29, 1864.

Over 1,500 soldiers were killed or wounded that day in the 13 black regiments that charged the enemy. Eight of the Medal of Honor winners were sergeants who led their companies into battle after all their white officers were killed or wounded.

A total of 1,354 men served in the 54th. One hundred of these were killed on the battlefield or died later of their wounds, 19 died of disease or accidents, and 57 were reported missing. Most of the missing were probably killed in places where it was impossible to search for their bodies. One hundred and fifty-eight of the men were discharged because they were disabled on the battlefield.

By the time the war ended, black soldiers had fought in 449 engagements, including at least 39 major battles.

"Without the military help of black freed men," President Lincoln declared, "the war against the South could not have been won."

The majority of the men who served were from slave states, since that's where most black people lived, and many of their families remained in slavery while the men fought. In the loyal border states, slavery continued to be legally protected by the Union through most or all of the war.

The 13th Amendment abolishing slavery wasn't ratified until December 18, 1865, eight months after the war ended.

Black men were still not allowed to vote in any state when the war was over, though Lincoln had suggested that veterans be given that right. In 1868, after much debate and against the opposition of President Andrew Johnson, Congress ratified the 14th Amendment.

The amendment basically guaranteed that the ex-slaves would be given the same protections as other citizens: freedom of speech, right to trial by an impartial jury, and protection against cruel and unusual punishment and unreasonable search and seizure.

In 1870, Congress ratified the 15th Amendment, prohibiting denial of the vote "on account of race, color, or previous condition of servitude."

Some men from the 54th stayed in the South to teach after the war. Lieutenant Swails taught for the Freedmen's Bureau, which was established to help the ex-slaves in their transformation to life as free citizens. The bureau built over 4,000 schools for black people, creating the first widespread public school system in the South.

Sergeant Lewis Douglass also stayed in the South as a teacher. Some of his pupils were the same ones his father had secretly taught as a slave 40 years before, while others were their sons and daughters.

From 1870 to 1900, 22 black men were elected to Congress. Black political power fell rapidly, however, when federal troops were removed from the South in 1877.

With the troops gone, blacks were once again at

the mercy of violence. Black schools were burned down throughout the South, and teachers killed or run out of town.

Soon blacks were attacked and even killed if they tried to vote, and by 1900 black voters had been largely eliminated from the rolls of every Southern state.

The battle the men of the 54th and other black regiments had successfully waged on the battlefield was lost in state legislatures and Congress. With it, this country's first serious effort to resolve the problem of racial inequality was also lost, and future generations would be left to deal with it.

What the 54th ("Glory") Regiment and the others did would be forgotten for many decades, as if tens of thousands of black soldiers had never paid for freedom with their lives and with their blood.

In 1887, against a background of increasing racial violence, approximately 300 veterans of the 54th held a reunion in Boston. The veterans of Wagner, Olustee, and Honey Hill called on the government to use "every proper means and influence it may possess to see to it that the colored defenders of its life in its day of peril, and their kindred or race, have the full and equal protection of the laws."

Then they visited the grave of Governor Andrew, knowing they and their comrades had fulfilled the work he committed to them on that "fine and cloudless day" so many years before: "a work at once so proud, so precious, so full of hope and glory. . . .".

They also knew that largely because of their ful-fillment of that work, slavery had been abolished and the foundations laid for a nation where all men might one day live as equals.

Horace Greeley of the *New York Tribune*, writing within days of the regiment's return to Boston, told of the importance of its success for all Americans: "It is not too much to say that if this Massachusetts Fifty-fourth had faltered when its trial came, two hundred thousand colored troops for whom it was a pioneer would never have been put into the field, or would not have been put in for another year, which would have been equivalent to protracting the war. . . .

"When it started across that fatal beach which led to the parapet of Wagner, it started to do what had not been successfully attempted by white troops on either side during the war. It passed through such an ordeal successfully; it came out not merely with credit, but with an imperishable fame."

Today, so many years after the men of the 54th "rallied from the hillside and gathered from the plain," their fame shines brighter than ever.

Bibliography

Government Publications:

The Negro in the Military Service of the United States, 1639–1886. National Archives. Seven volumes. Volume 4 consists of telegrams, reports, letters, and other papers from the Civil War. Part of Records of the Adjutant General's Office, Record Group 94.

Books:

Berlin, Ira, ed. *Freedom: A Documentary History of Emancipation, 1861–1867. Series II: The Black Military Experience.* Cambridge: Cambridge University Press, 1982.

Bigglestone, William E. *They Stopped in Oberlin.* Scottsdale: Innovation Group Inc., 1981.

Brandt, Nat. *The Town That Started the Civil War.* Syracuse: Syracuse University Press, 1990.

Brown, William Wells. *The Negro in the American Rebellion: His Heroism and His Fidelity.* New York: Citadel Press, 1971. (Book was originally published in 1867.)

Burchard, Peter. *One Gallant Rush.* Toronto: Macmillan Co. of Canada, 1965.

Coffin, Charles C. *Four Years of Fighting: A Volume of Personal Observation with the Army and Navy.* Ticknor and Fields, 1866. Reprint, Salem: Arno Press, Inc., 1970.

Cornish, Dudley Taylor. *The Sable Arm: Black Troops in the Union Army, 1861–1865.* Lawrence: University Press of Kansas, 1987.

Douglass, Frederick. *Life and Times of Frederick Douglass.* Prineville: Bonanza Books, 1962.

Emilio, Luis E. *A Brave Black Regiment: History of the Fifty-fourth Regiment of Massachusetts Volunteer Infantry, 1863–1865.* Boston: Boston Book Company, 1894. Johnson Reprint Corp., 1968.

Foner, Eric. *Reconstruction: America's Unfinished Revolution, 1863–1877.* New York: Harper & Row, 1988.

Foner, Jack D. *Blacks and the Military in American History.* New York: Praeger Publishers, Inc., 1974.

Foner, Philip S. *History of Black Americans: From the Compromise of 1850 to the End of the Civil War.* New York: Greenwood Press, 1983.

Franklin, John Hope. *From Slavery to Freedom.* New York: Alfred A. Knopf, 1967.

Glatthaar, Joseph T. *Forged in Battle: The Civil War Alliance of Black Soldiers and White Officers.* New York: The Free Press, 1990.

Higginson, Thomas Wentworth. *Army Life in a Black Regiment.* Boston: Fields, Osgood & Co., 1870. Reprint, Time-Life in 1982.

Katz, William Loren. *Eyewitness: The Negro in American History.* New York: Pittman Publishing Corp., 1974.

Lader, Lawrence. *The Bold Brahmins: New England's War*

Against Slavery, 1831–1863. New York: E.P. Dutton & Co., Inc., 1961.

Livermore, Mary. *My Story of the War.* 1890. Reprinted by Arno Press, Inc., 1972, from a copy in the Wesleyan University Library.

Livermore, Thomas L. *Numbers and Losses in the Civil War in America, 1861–1865.* Bloomington: Indiana University Press, 1957.

McPherson, James M. *The Struggle for Equality: Abolitionists and the Negro in the Civil War and Reconstruction.* Princeton: Princeton University Press, 1964.

———. *The Negro's Civil War.* New York: Pantheon Books, 1965.

———. *Battle Cry of Freedom: The Civil War Era.* New York: Ballantine Books, 1988.

Nolty, Bernard C. *Strength for the Fight: A History of Black Americans in the Military.* New York: The Free Press, 1986.

Pauli, Hertha. *Her Name Was Sojourner.* Englewood Cliffs: Appleton-Century-Crofts, 1962.

Quarles, Benjamin. *The Negro in the Civil War.* New York: Da Capo Press, 1989.

Ross, Ishbel. *Angel of the Battlefield: The Life of Clara Barton.* New York: Harper & Row, 1956.

Singletary, Otis. *The Negro Militia and Reconstruction.* New York: McGraw-Hill, 1963.

Sterling, Dorothy. *The Making of an Afro-American: Martin Robinson Delaney.* New York: Doubleday & Co., 1971.

———. *Speak Out in Thunder Tones: Letters and Other Writings by Black Northerners, 1787–1865.* New York: Doubleday & Co., 1973.

Sterling, Philip, and Logan, Rayford, eds. *Four Took Freedom: The Lives of Harriet Tubman, Frederick Douglass, Robert Smalls, and Blanche K. Bruce.* New York: Doubleday & Co., 1967.

Trumbull, H. Clay. *War Memories of an Army Chaplain.* New

York: Charles Scribner's Sons, 1898. An original copy from
the New York State Library in Albany was used.

Voegeli, Jacque. *Free But Not Equal: The Midwest and the Negro
during the Civil War.* Chicago: University of Chicago Press,
1970.

Wilson, Joseph T. *The Black Phalanx: A History of the Negro
Soldiers of the United States in the Wars of 1775, 1812, 1861–
1865.* Reprint, Arno Press, Inc. 1968.

Periodicals:

Aptheker, Herbert. "Negro Casualties in the Civil War." *Journal of Negro History*, Vol. XXXII (January 1947), pp. 10–
80.

Blassingame, John W. "Negro Chaplains in the Civil War."
Negro History Bulletin (October 1963), pp. 23–24.

Harper's Weekly. (August 15, 1863). Article on Colonel Shaw
and the attack on Fort Wagner, p. 526.

Heller, Charles E. "Between Two Fires: The 54th Massachusetts." *Civil War Times Illustrated*, Vol. II (April 1972), pp.
33–41.

Levy, Leonard W. "Sims' Case: The Fugitive Slave Law in
Boston in 1851." *Journal of Negro History*, Vol. XXXV (January 1950), pp. 39–74.

Reddick, L.D. "The Negro Policy of the United States Army,
1775–1945." *Journal of Negro History*, Vol. XXXIV (January
1949), pp. 9–29.

Shannon, Fred A. "The Federal Government and the Negro
Soldier, 1861–1865." *Journal of Negro History*, Vol. XI (October 1926), pp. 563–583.

Woodson, Carter G., ed. "A Social Experiment: The Port
Royal Journal of Charlotte L. Forten, 1862–1863." *Journal of Negro History*, Vol. XXXV, No. 3 (July 1950),
pp. 233–264.

————, ed. "Documents." *Journal of Negro History*, Vol. XI (January 1926) Letters from Lewis Douglass and letters from residents of Philadelphia describing Frederick Douglass' recruiting activities in that city, pp. 83–84, 95.

Newspapers:

Douglass's Monthly. March, April, June, and August, 1863. Describes issues facing black Americans and tells about activities of the 54th, including their departure from Camp Meigs.

Lorain County News, Ohio, April 15, June 24, August 5, September 2, 1863. Letters and information about Henry Peal and other Oberlin residents in the 54th.

The New York Times, April 4, 1865. Article describing the triumphant parade of Union soldiers through Charleston, South Carolina, along with firemen, sailors, and many of the ex-slaves.

The New York Times, August 3, 1887. Brief article describing reunion of black Union veterans in Boston, and their visit to the grave of Governor Andrew.

*   *   *

Microfilm of *Douglass's Monthly* courtesy of the New York State Public Library, Albany, New York. Microfilm of the *Lorain County News* courtesy of the Oberlin College Library, Oberlin, Ohio.

Index